Education and Empowering Backward Minorities

Education and Empowering Backward Minorities

Education and Empowering Backward Minorities

A. Basheer

SHIPRA

Rs. 850

ISBN: 978-93-86262-21-9

First Published in India in 2017

Education and Empowering Backward Minorities

Published by:

SHIPRA PUBLICATIONS
LG 18-19, Pankaj Central Market,
I.P. Ext., Patparganj, Delhi 110092, India
Ph.: +91 11 22235152/6152

Foreword

Education is the most enlightening and empowering aspect of human society. It has been changing its pattern with change in the pattern of society. From ancient times knowledge has been accumulating and being disseminated through various mechanisms. Later, it also got associated with religion and took the form of seminaries, madrassas and gurukuls, etc. With the renaissance, modern science coming in the pattern of knowledge, system of education took a giant leap. In education, one aspect relates to overall development of one's perception of the World around and the other is the one which makes one capable of enhancing one's life, preparing for a gainful employment. The very process of literacy adds to the process of empowerment of people in the society. The goals of education in society are multifarious and also depend on the agenda of the ruling governments in various countries.

In India, the modern education was introduced by the British to create a class of people who could be utilized in the British administration. So, the goals were very narrow and served the interests of the rulers. This also unleashed a process which was beyond the goals of the British. The unanticipated goal was the broad increase in general awareness of the people all over the country. This also brought them in touch with the global philosophies and knowledge systems. Initially, the education was restricted to the elite, later with the efforts of people like Jotirao Phule and Savitribai Phule, the deepening of the process amongst average people started coming in. In India — a multi-religious, multi-ethnic nation — the process of education was not uniform.

Amongst Muslims, the largest minority community in India, the introduction of education had different challenges.

Large sections of Indian Muslims come from low caste background, so economic deprivation was inherent among this community. Adding on to the problem was the British singling out Muslims as the cause of 1857 rebellion. They undertook to punish large number of Muslims and kept them away from the process of administrative jobs. This malady of Muslim community was well identified by Sir Syed Ahmad Khan, who undertook extraordinary measures to ensure that Muslims become recipients of Modern education and thereby also enter the administrative occupations in due course. Still his initiatives were restricted to the elite Muslims. The larger section of Muslim community remained deprived from the process and also was kept away from the other accompaniments which follow the educational attainments.

At the time of independence the status of education among Muslim community was abysmal. Dalits were also situated on the lower rungs of society as far as education is concerned. Due to the affirmative action of state in the form of reservations a section of Dalits started coming in to the field of education and jobs, lifting their condition partly. The plight of Muslims got worst confounded as the communal forces started targeting them as the one's responsible for partition of the country and blamed them for formation of Pakistan, which as such was a complex phenomenon. Formation of Pakistan really was due to British policy of divide and rule assisted by the role of Hindu and Muslim communal organizations. As the jobs were by and large denied to Muslim community, the incentive for education was very little and so the overall spread and reach of education to Muslim masses remained poor all through. The direct relation of education-literacy with the government and other private jobs and family size is abundantly obvious. The fact was brought to social attention by different commissions like Gopal Singh (1981), Sachar Committee (2006), Rangnath Mishra Commission (2007).

With the process of globalization coming in from the decade of 1990s, the matters started worsening as the state gradually started withdrawing from the social sectors of education and health. The result was that education started becoming commercialized and privatized; through and through. It meant that only those who are affluent can have access to education while other less privileged has to fend for them. The impact of this was clear on the poorer sections of society and Muslims have been the worst victims. Large sections of Muslims remain on the margins of society due to the lack of education and insecurity created due to communal violence. It is in these circumstances that large number of poor Muslims have to continue to depend on Madrassa education even today.

Kerala is one of the most progressive states in the country, a state which has achieved universal literacy, a rare feet in the Indian context. Kerala Muslims' while being in substantial number are still a minority and victims of many a biases and stereotypes which operate at National level. The process of privatization and commercialization has a very adverse effect on the Kerala Muslim community as is the general observation that such privatization is detrimental to the interests of poorer sections.

It is in this backdrop that Dr. A. Basheer's "Education and Empowering Backward Minorities" becomes an important initiative to understand the social phenomenon which is related to privatization of education. The work is very topical and based on impeccable research and methodically painstaking field work. In today's scenario where the communal forces are making a quick ascendance in Kerala, such a work should help the policy-makers, institutions working in the field of education to plan their future course of action as far as education among the Muslim community is concerned. I am sure such work will greatly help the social workers and researchers to understand the social milieu better so that their interventions can be more precise and meaningful. While complimenting Dr. Basheer for his valuable contribution to the body of knowledge relevant for social change, I do hope better policies will be undertaken in the future for the overall empowerment of the society at large and Muslim community in particular.

Ram Puniyani
Centre for Study of Society and Secularism,
Mumbai.

Acknowledgments

The quest to understand the implications of private provision of education service for the empowerment of the backward and disadvantaged sections of the population, particularly the minority communities, was the motivation in undertaking the present study. Research to simulate and weave coherently the views and perceptions of people at different levels of understanding of socio-economic and political realities is often arduous and painstaking. Although, the role of the private sector in providing education service to the public cannot be underplayed, apprehensions of people in the context of globalisation and its prescriptions of liberalisations, privatisation and marketisation/commercialisation of public services is certainly a matter of concern to the public, particularly the disadvantaged sections. This, perhaps, has been a factor that pondered in my thought while deciding to consider a study on the problem of private provision of education.

I owe my debt to the UGC that awarded me a major research project which yielded the present academic exercise.

My warmest gratitude is for Dr. G. Gopakumar, (presently Vice-Chancellor, Central University of Kerala) who provided guidance from the very beginning and his intellectual support was immensely useful in this work. C. Muraleedharan, Dr. J. Prabhash, Dr. Shajivarkey, Dr. Sajad Ibrahim and Dr. Joskutty Abraham were very supportive mentors who sustained my confidence. The invigorating interactions with these people benefitted me a lot as I gained useful insights.

G.N. Panikkar, eminent Professor of English, a prolific writer and former Director of Public Relations and Cultural Affairs

Department, Government of Kerala, deserves my appreciation for his excellent editorial inputs in improving the product.

Shri Ram Puniyani is a widely popular defender of human rights, a steadfast crusader of Dalit issues and a supporter of secularism. My request to write a foreword for this book was responded by him well ahead of my expectations. I do express my deep and sincere gratitude to him.

I do recognise the valuable services rendered by Miss Lija, Research Fellow, in conducting field survey and related works. And I express my sincere gratitude to all who extended their direct or indirect help in completing this work.

Dr. A. Basheer

Abbreviations

AICTE	All India Council for Technical Education
EER	Eligible Enrolment Rate
GDP	Gross Domestic Product
GER	General Enrolment Rate
ICESCR	International Covenant on Economic, Social and Cultural Rights
MDG	Millennium Development Goals
MES	Muslim Education Society
NEP	New Education Policy
NPE	New Policy of Education
NSS	Nair Service Society
NSS	National Sample Survey
OBC	Other Backward Community
SC	Scheduled Caste
SNDP	Sree Narayana Dharma Paripalana Yogam
SSA	Sarva Siksha Abhiyan
ST	Scheduled Tribe
UDHR	Universal Declaration of Human Rights
UEE	Universal Elementary Education
UGC	University Grants Commission
UNDHR	United Nations Universal Declaration of Human Rights
UNESCO	United Nations Educational Scientific and Cultural Organisation
UNHD	United Nations Human Development (Report)
UNMD	United Nations Millennium Declaration
US	United States
UPA	United Progressive Alliance

Contents

1
Introduction

Being part of our social life and serving a vital role in it, education reflects a society's fundamental assumptions about itself and the individuals who constitute it, and enables one to discover and achieve a purpose in life.[1] Only education can imbue people with the knowledge, a sense of purpose and the confidence essential for building a dynamic, vibrant and cohesive nation capable of providing its people with the resources for creating better and purposeful life. Educated people, by gaining understanding of the community in which they live, can chart a course of their own to fulfill their needs and empower themselves by taking responsibility for their own and the community's progress and by gaining greater control over their lives as socially responsible individuals.

Education is considered as the most potential means for human development, a means to elevate persons by helping them realise the ability to contribute effectively to nation-building and societal development. The Report of the Education Commission (1964-66) linked education to the task of nation-building and the development project. According to the Commission, "In a world based on science and technology it is education that determines the level of prosperity, welfare and security of people." The standard of living of people depends on the quality and number of persons educated. Education can enrich human life and shape human destiny, equip men to determine their own destiny, give them security and advantages, make them confident, autonomous, dignified, curious, critical, constructive, creative and caring, audacious, basically optimistic despite difficulties and sufferings.[2] It could help children transform into free human beings. Education operates as a multiplier, enhancing the enjoyment of all individual rights and freedoms.

Levels of education attainment in societies correlate strongly with a vast array of important variables in the human development process."[3] Communities and nations develop relative to what they accomplish in education. Education is insurance for individual and community progress. *Dakar Declaration* has stated, "No country can be expected to develop into a modern and open economy without a certain proportion of its workforce having completed secondary education."[4] Deprivation of education impinges on the life chances of individuals.

Educated people become organised and acquire the potential to overcome alienation, marginalisation and powerlessness. Alienated citizens who remain passive, disengaged, withdrawn and inactive in socio-political spheres would be invigorated and encouraged to be active, efficacious and involved and engaged in public sphere. Members of the socially and economically backward classes will be enabled to get into positions of power, public employment and other walks of public life and help them to elevate their position in society shedding their earlier inferior status through education. Education and economic well-being of an individual give him/her a dignified status in society. All these are requirements for empowerment of the individual. Thus education enables people to attain resources for empowerment. Hence, education is a critical part of wider empowerment process through which people can exercise greater control over their lives and over the well-being of their family members, community and the nation. Improvement in perceived and actual ability to control is essence of empowerment. Empowerment of individuals depends on restoration to them of a sense of values and strength and capacity to handle life's problems. Empowerment of the students/citizens who take responsibility for their own and their community's and country's progress is one of the core objectives of education. Here education is viewed as a tool to empower the students/citizens to be effective and active in the mainstream of social affairs. People gaining self-sufficiency so as to self-support by developing skills, and removing the disabilities they suffer from and the conditions that foster powerlessness in life situations is crucial in this respect.

Empowerment is crucial for progress of weaker sections, especially minorities in any society. Only through empowerment can they be liberated from structures of exploitation, oppression, discrimination, subordination, dependence, servitude etc. The situations that weaken empowerment of minorities – feeling of marginality, inferiority, lower-self-esteem, powerlessness and iniquitous power relations between dominant sections and minority groups need be removed. The welfare, social justice and empowerment of the disadvantaged and marginalised sections can be achieved by bringing them from the periphery into the mainstream of development by making them self-reliant, increasing their self-confidence, self-respect and self-esteem. They need be integrated into the social, political, economic and cultural process. Education and economic and political measures are crucial for this. Therefore, education is recognized as a basic, inalienable right that must be guaranteed in all human societies. The Supreme Court of India has interpreted Article 45 of the Constitution to serve as a legal source for a claim to education, lending strength to the demand for a right to education. This culminated in the 93rd Constitutional amendment in 2001 which granted education the status of a fundamental right with the constitutional guarantee that the state shall provide free and compulsory education to all children in the age group of 6-14.

Education is an empowerment right which enables all persons and communities to transcend poverty and obtain the means to participate fully and effectively in community life. Therefore, all individuals have the human right to benefit from an education that will meet their basic learning needs, and that seeks to tap and develop each individual's talents, potential and personalities, so that they can 'improve their lives and transform their societies'.[5]

More and equal opportunities for education need be availed to all for this purpose. The goal of inclusive education envisages providing more affordable educational opportunities to those who are most educationally backward in the country. The educational institutions should be open and accessible equally to all sections of society so as to ensure affordable and equitable distribution of education and remove educational inequality between communities. In a world that requires knowledge and skills, there is public rationale for education to ensure individual, social, public and community benefits and empower the poor, backward and disenfranchised to change their communities and improve their lives.

The state has to play a powerful role in educating the whole people, the masses, particularly the children of poverty, ignorance and disadvantages. Almost everywhere government has been the principal provider of education with the objective of equipping the young generation with the necessary skills they need to escape poverty and unemployment. Encompassing equal social conditions (education is a core social condition), is the responsibility of democratic government.

Since education, notwithstanding all its positive features, is also connected more widely with power and social inequality,[6] it is important to prevent a distorted education system which denies access to the disadvantaged sections in the society which adversely affects their empowerment. Inequality in distribution of educational resources, education success and employment opportunities and income, all distorting factors in empowerment of the disadvantaged sections must be removed. In the privatized education environment, the problem of 'different education/school systems reproducing social inequalities'[7] must be effectively addressed.

Education and empowerment of minority communities is a problem faced by governments all over the world, especially countries inhabited by a plurality of communities. Minority communities in many countries nourish the grievance with regard to poor allocation of public funds and other facilities for the education of their members. UNESCO is much concerned with this problem and devotes considerable resources for this.

Education and empowerment of the Muslim community in Kerala, the largest minority community in the state, constituting 24.7 per cent of its population, and enumerated within the category of Socially and Educationally Backward Classes suffering relative deprivation in the field of education as well as in different spheres and in terms of levels of living and human development conditions, has been a challenge for the government and the community.

A number of factors including socio-economic development lag, historical and social prejudices and de facto segregation/exclusion tended to impede the attainment of equality of opportunity for minority Muslim children in the educational context.

Socio-religious status and economic backwardness significantly affected the community's ability to advance education participation and attainment, although the upper echelons in the community like that of other higher classes who are privileged with high levels of social as well as cultural capital manage to score higher participation. The economic backwardness in terms of the inability to access equal opportunity in education and employment and extreme powerlessness and human development problems are key concerns of the community.

The community as such was constrained in effectively participating in the mainstream of socio-political, economic and cultural processes, and was not able to secure to its members social and economic opportunities to advance equality and justice and improve their living conditions.

Neglected/abandoned by the mainstream society, in fact, the community remained in the periphery being socially alienated, economically marginalised, and, politically and administratively excluded, with little self-respect and dignity vis-a-vis members of other advanced and forward communities. Freedom, dignity and well-being of the community were at low level.

Proper and rational education will enable them to get empowered and help in development of abilities to overcome powerlessness. Education of individual members will contribute to individual empowerment which will lead to community empowerment. Self-efficacy may become collective efficacy if it gets translated into the community's practical ability to organise itself for a collective effort to achieve outcomes in the environment, and ability to achieve outcomes to control their lives, to participate in decision-making, and to influence the environment. Otherwise the uneducated youth among the community are likely to be exploited by vested interests/religious fanatics or extremist groups. Moreover, lack of education will deprive them of equal opportunities and deny them social justice. Inequality will increase creating discontent.

In the context of large scale privatisation of education which renders education a tradable commodity and weakens public education thereby posing a challenge to the goal of equitable and inclusive education, the education and empowerment of minority Muslim community is a major challenge.

Since 1990s, the state of Kerala has been experiencing a mushrooming increase in the number of private educational institutions which are run by collecting prohibitively exorbitant rates of fees including capitation fee, beyond the prescribed norm, in surreptitious and unjust ways from students, without providing even minimum competent faculty strength. Inordinate majority of private institutions are 'surrogate businesses' which benefit little for majority of students who have poor socio-economic background. When the government opened the doors for large scale private investment in the sector, it was claimed that it was a measure to help the large number of students to find the educational opportunities of their choice in the state itself. Policy declarations in this respect averred that the principles of equity and social justice that had been the cornerstone of the State's education sector until then would continue to guide it in the new era of large-scale private investment too.

In the contemporary educational scenario defined by neo-liberal ideological underpinnings and extended private sector ambience, where popular education–education for all–is a challenge, the problem of education and empowerment of one of the largest minority communities in Kerala who were denied equal access to education which was communalist (in the pre-independent era) in character needed further investigation and detailed analysis.

In this process many questions are raised regarding the impact of privatisation of education on the empowerment of the backward sections among the population, particularly the members of the Muslim community. Related questions like what access difficulties/limitations the people face in a privatised education system?; to what extent do the people who seek education from private institutions score in social development or high level of participation in social, political, economic and cultural process?; to what extent the sense of powerlessness among the members of the Muslim community has been brought down?; to what level the community members have enhanced political efficacy or civic competence?; has bossism, dependency been eliminated?; whether members of the community have been transformed to be autonomous, confident, critical individuals to help themselves and control their life, destiny and environment? are also raised to focus on the inquiry.

This inquiry assumes significance, especially in the context of Kerala's internationally acclaimed achievements viz. universal primary education, near total literacy and near gender equality in access to education and commendable Human Development Index.

Objectives

The present study was undertaken to examine the extent to which privatization of education: (1) helped empowerment of the minority communities, especially the backward Muslim community and those who are at lower socio-economic level, and the nature of empowerment attained by them; change in enrolment and dropout rates of Muslim students, especially females against males in primary, secondary and higher education, including professional education; (2) helped the various sections within the Muslim community to secure basic rights, well-being, social equity and social justice leading to empowerment also in relation to members of other forward communities; (3) forged the crucible of civic capacity, improvement in performance standard and global competence of the members of the Muslim Community; and (4) helped in the promotion of the constitutional objectives of social justice and equity and social integration and an efficient mass of human capital in the Muslim community in Kerala — key to their empowerment.

The study proceeded with the following hypotheses:

1. Privatization of education defined by neo-liberal ideology and market principles weakens public education and tends to deny the poor backward sections among the minority communities equal access opportunities to education and educational participation, but facilitates increased participation of the privileged sections in education to gain stock of education. This system tends to widen intra-community as well as inter-community inequality in society. Poor minority communities suffer marginalization which impinges on their empowerment.
2. The expansion of education facilities via privatization avails educational opportunities to the minorities as well, but not equality. It is predominantly the privileged who acquire higher and professional quality education availed by private sector which hardly helps in the socio-economic mobility of less privileged within the community, nor does it serve public interest, nor result in the empowerment of the Muslim community as such.

3. The privileged among the Muslim community pursue higher education as employment/status/prestige enhancement device. Such goal setting hardly results in the empowerment of the community as a whole.
4. Privatization of education will exacerbate inequality which tends to reinforce powerlessness among the poor backward Muslim population. Powerless and backward position of most of rural Muslim population will lead to their further marginalization lowering their dignity and self-esteem.

Methodology

A combination of empirical and descriptive method with historical support was adopted for this exercise. For collection of primary data survey among 800 households, spread across four districts in Kerala viz. Kannur, Malappuram, Palghat and Trivandrum, where there is substantial presence of Muslim population and which represent areas with varying social, cultural and religious background, was conducted. 200 households from each district, spread in four Panchayats were selected on a random basis for the survey. Besides, about 100 persons from the Muslim community who are active in education field and social and political sphere were also interviewed with the help of interview schedule. Many academicians, public persons involved in or associated with the education field were also consulted, which helped to gain much insight into the problems and identify major issues pertaining to the subject of study.

Plan of Work

The work is divided into five chapters besides introduction and conclusion. In the first chapter a discussion on the nature of education, importance, principal functions, role in human development and social change and role as a tool of empowerment is attempted. The second chapter examines the concept of empowerment and its dimensions from a theoretical perspective. The third chapter is an investigation into the socio-economic profile and educational status of the Muslim community in Kerala who are socially and educationally backward, while the fourth chapter analyses the education policy of Kerala in the context of developments at the global and national levels. The fifth chapter considers the impact of privatisation of education on the empowerment of the Muslim community in Kerala from different perspectives, examining the advancement the community has been able to achieve in numerous parameters within which empowerment takes place.

Notes and References

1. Lindsay, Scrap book, 22, quoting CE Raven (2009), 'A Wanderer's Way,' 1928, in Alan Macfarlane, Reflections on Cambridge, Social Science Press, New Delhi, p. 187.
2. Tariq Ramadan (2010), 'The Quest for Meaning: Developing a Philosophy of Pluralism', Penguin, London, p. 131.
3. Janet R. Dickson *et al.*, (Eds.), *Advancing Global Education: Patterns of Potential Human Progress*, Vol. 2, Oxford, New Delhi, p. 159.
4. UNESCO 2000:16.
5. Education for All: Meeting Our Collective Commitments, Text adopted by the World Education Forum, Dakar, Senegal, April 26-28, 2000.
6. Sharon Gewitz and Alan Cribb (2009), 'Understanding Education: A Sociological Perspective', Polity Press, Cambridge, p. 41.
7. *Ibid.*, p. 41.

2

Education and its Role in Society

Education, widely valued for it, and considered as the greatest blessing bestowed upon mankind, next to life and liberty is part of our social life, and is the one universal principle common to all spiritualities, religions, philosophies, civilizations and cultures. As a process of teaching, training and learning to improve knowledge and develop skills[1], education is central to giving humans' the knowledge and skills to make informed decisions and acquire better health, better living standards and safer, more sustainable environments. It enables us to know (acquire the instruments of understanding), to do, (so as to be able to act creatively in one's environment), to live together, (so as to participate and cooperate with other people in all human activities) and to be. UNESCO's report of the International Commission on Education for the 21st century suggests education to be organised around the above mentioned four fundamental types of learning: the four pillars of knowledge.

Education is for life, cultivation of responsible citizenship and to help the people learn how to cope with the society. It plays a vital role in human development, accords continuity to intellect, knowledge and values, and promotes methodical and inventive development of the intelligence of the students so that they will gain adjustability and success in the world. Education is a total business of head, heart, spirit and body.[2] An educated individual develops his potential to the full, develops power of mind and cultivates the right interests, attitudes and intellectual and moral values. John Locke, in his *Some Thoughts Concerning Education* argues that 'man is not just a mind but also a body that must be properly trained and educated. Hence education is about enhancing human capabilities. It enhances our freedom and creativity and insures the progress of the individual and community. It signifies for many a desperate means of coping with the intensely competitive highly uncertain global situation. It is socially important as it distributes academic credentials which give access to other socially and economically, culturally and politically valued goods. Education really promises public benefits in the form of economic growth, political coherence, community's cultural advancement, and social order. Moulding a generation, education also reflects a society's fundamental assumptions about itself and the individuals which constitute it.

Hence, education is considered as a basic inalienable right that must be guaranteed in all human societies. General Comment 13 of the International Covenant of Economic, Social and Cultural Rights considers education as an end in itself and a means for realising other rights, operating as a multiplier and enhancing the enjoyment of all individual rights and freedoms. These rights foster the non-derogable right to life, which is the foundation of all rights. Along with right to food and primary health, it is identified as important to the realisation of the right to development.

Education in Islam

Islam accords very important place for education in the development of both males and females, particularly young children. According to Islamic view education concerns all the people. Different people have different concerns in education. Islam recognises the centrality of education in providing knowledge and skills to people to enable them to lead better living standards. The first word revealed of Quran was 'Iqra'-read, seek knowledge, educate yourself and be educated. Islam encourages the seeking of all types of knowledge – academic, vocational, religious and secular – at all ages. Prophet Mohammed considered knowledge as the most important thing directly concerned with human life. For him knowledge was treasure. Without knowledge man can fall much astray from right path and may be misled. He is like someone walking along a track in complete darkness. Most likely, his steps will wander aside and he easily can be deceived. And our greatest danger lies in our ignorance. Hence, a Muslim cannot live in a state of ignorance. Therefore, seeking knowledge is considered a sacred duty, obligatory on every Muslim. Acquiring knowledge is worship; travelling to gain knowledge is worship. The practice of knowledge is connected with ethics and morality, with promoting virtue and combating vice, enjoying right and forbidding wrong. Knowledge must be linked with values. Purpose of knowledge is to spread freedom and dignity, truth and justice, and gain the good of this world, not to destroy it nor to gain power and dominance.

Explaining the meaning of theory of education in Islam, Allama Iqbal mentions, "The fostering of self, training, wakefulness, construction and stability in fundamental principles".[3] Education is one critical aspect of nation-building process that introduces skills and knowledge that are useful for the construction and creativity of native/community institutions through which people can realise their values, culture and interests.

Muslim education is proposed to be shaped so as to provide guidance to the individual from what he is to what he should be.[4] Education, in fact, has much to do with the transmission of a value system, behavioural norms and elements of culture as with the transmission of skills and knowledge.

In Islam, education is actually related to soul and spirit…., to intellect and wisdom which differentiated human beings from other creatures and included all activities which make the life of human beings organized, useful, and cultured; and to body which is concerned with the existence, security and progressive aspects of the body.

Gandhian Education

Gandhi laid the foundation of a scheme of national education that was suited to our needs, requirements, genius and aspirations for the future. His system of education was an alternative to the system introduced by the British colonial system which, he believed, was to a great extent faulty and detrimental, and caused prolongation of the period of our helplessness. Gandhiji declared that English education of Macaulay was irrelevant to the country's context; it alienated the student from his motherland and culture, and did not make him vocationally any worthier.

Gandhiji's education was nationalist in setting, idealist in nature, and pragmatic with social purpose and spiritual intention, and has social significance. Considered as a means to guide and lead a human being from his birth to death, it works for the all-round growth of a man. It emphasised the highest development of mind and soul. Gandhiji desired complete physical and mental development of man through value education. According to him, it is only through education that men become human beings. He believed that without education a human being is not different from an animal. The role of a university or other educational institution is to foster these goals. Proper and harmonious combination of intellect, body and heart and soul is required for the making of the whole man – and that constitutes true economics of education.

Gandhiji would prefer school to be a *brahmacharya ashram* where students live the life of *brahmacharies*, practising spiritual discipline. According to him true education enables us to preserve our *dharma* (religion) and serve others and oblige them without the least feeling of one-apishness. And education is to inspire the children with a new ideology based upon personal purity and unselfish service, resulting in the creation of a society grounded on truth and love. To do good to others and serve them without any sense of egoism – this is the real education.

For Gandhiji education should contemplate the whole life. Learning to live a good life is education in itself rest is useless.[5] He emphasised an education for life, education through life, and education throughout life. The act of instilling life into the education process is the solution for any kind of educational development for our country. That education alone is of value which draws out the faculties of a student so as to enable him or her to solve correctly the problems of life in every department.[6] The aim of education is to turn human knowledge into his ability and make his life worthy and meaningful. For Gandhiji, imparting education among the children should aim at preparing them in the specific knowledge, skills and abilities that can be applied in life. In his scheme, higher education was to perform the essential function of providing training and properly motivating human power for national needs. In dynamic societies, education has to equip individuals with the skills and attitudes necessary for them to adapt to changing conditions, and for constructive participation in the task of social change. It instils courage and self-reliance in the individuals, and helps them cultivate the highest intellectual, moral and ethical accomplishments.

Gandhiji emphasised individual's self-reliance, which could pave the way for his true development. Becoming efficient, skilful and self-reliant, one could tread on the pathway to progress and could contribute to the society, nation and the world.

That the concept of life has been taken away from education is precisely the reason for the dehumanising, alienating aspect of education. Over and above acquiring knowledge, the more important thing is to learn humanity. Education should be intimately related to human experience. The primary function of teacher, rather then teaching the alphabet, is to inculcate humanity. True education is that which helps us to know the atman, our true self.

For Gandhiji education must draw out the best from children. Gandhiji had attached great importance to primary education, and considered imparting it to the people of India as a great strength for the nation. He preferred adult education to have an intensive programme of driving out ignorance.

For Gandhiji, education was an essential instrument for materialising his dream of Sarvodaya Samaj in which the vertical and horizontal distance between people is reduced to a minimum. This scheme of education was geared up to checking the progressive decay of villages, reviving the village economy, laying the foundation of a just social order, in which there is no unnatural division between the 'haves' and the 'have-nots' and everybody is assured of achieving acceptable standards. The basic educational scheme was an essential ingredient of his plan to eliminate the rural-urban divide and redress the structural and socio-economic imbalances that hovers the Indian society. Gandhiji regarded his scheme of education as spearheading the silent social revolution and expected it to provide a healthy relationship between the city and the village, which would go a long way in eradicating the poisoned relationship between the classes. It had its goal to achieve freedom from servitude and freedom from domination to one's own artificial needs. His concept of basic education formulated in the context of poverty, illiteracy, backwardness, frustration and the degeneration of the masses resulting from the disruption of traditional social institutions and destruction of the small scale cottage industry was intended to address those issues. It stood for a new outlook, a new approach. He wrote in the *Harijan*, "Education must be of a new type for the sake of the creation of a new world".[7]

Gandhiji insisted that work and knowledge must never be separated. The education that integrates work and knowledge helps children break down existing barriers of prejudice between manual and intellectual workers. Separation of learning (knowledge) from labour results in social injustices, and has been the fountain-head of all the conflicts in the world. Therefore, what Gandhiji proposed was a system that had the maximum possible capacity of self-support from people's work experience which is both an instrument of education and a source of income. Basic Education sought to incorporate manual work or hands-on experience of productive craft in the core curriculum of primary schools. It was based on the assumption that the hands-on experience of making or doing something serves multiple developmental purposes in children's lives. Given the caste framework of the Indian society which legitimises derision for manual work by linking it with lower castes and others stigmatised by exclusion from the hierarchy of castes, this was a revolutionary idea.

Real education does not consist merely in acquainting oneself with books or acquiring a stock of knowledge from them, but in the habits one imbibes from the atmosphere, one's surroundings and the company one keeps and above all in work. Literacy in itself is no education but only one of the means whereby men can be educated in the above sense.

Functions of Education

1. Generation of Knowledge and Transmission of Values

Education is a key site of knowledge production and provides an opportunity for people (predominantly young) to be inducted into the cultures and practices of knowledge production. World Bank acknowledged that institutions of education have the main responsibility for equipping individuals with advanced knowledge and skills required for positions of responsibility.[8] To educate means something more than passing on information; it is largely experienced in a struggle to absorb, reshape and transmit ideas and develop critical thinking-knowledge. Schools play a critical role in equipping children with knowledge and skills that provide social and economic opportunities. The knowledge and skills the individual gain through education is necessary for him to take control of his own life. He will be self-determining in achieving self-efficacy and empowerment.

Kothari Commission Report highlighted the principal objective of universities as "to deepen man's understanding of the universe and of himself – in body, mind and spirit, to disseminate this understanding throughout society and to apply it in the service of mankind." Indian universities are envisaged to seek and cultivate new knowledge, engage vigorously and fearlessly in the pursuit of truth and interpret old knowledge and belief in the light of new needs and discoveries. Tariq Ramadan explains, "Education shapes an understanding of the world, affects values, and therefore, alters human behaviour. And schools and the process of education deliberately transmits society's accumulated knowledge, skills and values, value systems, behavioural norms and elements of culture to the succeeding generations.[9]

2. *Character Building*

The right type of education builds up character. Education's functions of transmission of values, behavioural norms and elements of culture, knowledge and the skills, influences character-building in individuals. It is a pre-condition for man's humanity.

"Education will produce individuals who are self-confident, autonomous, dignified, curious, critical, constructive, creative and caring."[10] Education partly shapes the personal identity of the student. "Diligent men, direct men, independent, loving men– these are what schools must turn out".[11] It is rightly observed that 'education is a total business of head, heart, spirit and body'. [12]

Schools can foster attitudes based on mutual respect, shared interest and common values, helping to underpin social cohesion in culturally diverse societies, or can promote ideas and practices that weaken cohesion.[13] In "The School Class as a Social System" Talcott Parsons explores the role of (US) schools, both in socialising individuals into, and the norms and values he believes were demanded by society and in selecting them for and allocating them to their future social and economic roles. Parsons argues that there are certain structural features common to elementary schools which enable them to perform two crucial functions in the maintenance of social order. First, schools, alongside and in interaction with the family and the peer group, play a crucial role in shaping children's personalities and specifically their commitments and capacities in ways that equip them for performing their future adult roles as responsible citizens. Second, as children progress through the elementary school, they are increasingly differentiated from each other on the basis of a combination of their cognitive and moral achievements, that is, their capacity to act in accord with societal values.[14]

According to the UDHR and ICESCR, education should be directed at the full development of the human personality and the sense of its dignity, strengthening respect for human rights and fundamental freedoms and promotion of understanding, tolerance, friendship and peace. Bowles and Gintis emphasise that an 'adequate education system in a good society' should serve three purposes:

(i) promote personal development through the inculcation of appropriate knowledge and intellectual skills, as well as through developing 'those affective and interpersonal skills which allow individuals to control their own lives, and foster the self-esteem and personal dignity which lead them to demand the resources, to exercise such control;
(ii) 'act as an equalising force', disrupting rather than reproducing privilege and disadvantage; and
(iii) act as 'a stabilising force...[15] The essence of education is to help people to find themselves.

Prof. Kothari attached utmost significance to the character building role of education. In one of his addresses he said: if the character building role of education is properly recognized, making work experience an integral part of education will not be difficult. Work experience with its integration of mental, manual and moral elements should be an integral part of education at all stages.

Most important is to bring teachers and students to direct and meaningful contact with the life and needs, and, aspiration of the people especially the underprivileged. Without such a contact with the living world education loses much of its relevance and moral dimension. Kothari is of the view that "today the situation of the world is to small extent a result of 'bad education' — education divorced from values and character-building".

3. *Generation of Ideas*

Educational institutions are places where ideas are generated, contested and disseminated. Schools should be like houses of reason where with judicious guidance the child is accustomed to develop his own thinking, and objects and ideas are set before him in an orderly relationship.

Education fundamentally shapes culture – ideas, beliefs and values as well as social practices and relationships, the formal and informal institutions that build up on and perpetuate them. In much of the developing world education, in combination with economic and demographic change, is involved in a revolutionary reshaping of traditional cultures.[16] According to John Caldwell the adoption of western mass education throughout the world transforms cultures.[17]

4. *Preparing Students for Life*

Education is the shield for the battle of life. The main function/aim of education is to 'make the student fit for his historic moment and circumstance', prepare the pupil for life. The linguistic, cognitive and social skills children develop in early childhood are the foundations for lifelong learning. Hence it is suggested 'education should contemplate the whole life'. Through education students learn how to practice life in its true, social and moral sense. As Jose Marti, a Cuban writer, has stated, "school must be like a shop where the student may learn about the forces with which he will have to struggle later on".[18] The NEP of India (1968) sought to bring about a transformation of the education system to relate it more closely to the life of the people. A university does not make but form a man. It can make an individual determined to be a don in order not to lose the way of life.[19] It can enrich one's life; enormously give him security and advantages, equip man to be his own destiny and shape his own destiny. Since man's destiny is life, education must prepare him for living. Education makes people to become absolute masters of the world and of their own destiny by completely transforming nature, society and human beings themselves in accordance with the essential social quality of men who want to live and develop independently, and provides the means for achieving sustainable happiness and prosperity of mankind.

People who lack elementary knowledge will not be able to fulfil themselves either individually or socially. In the words of Marti, "knowing how to read is knowing how to walk/act. Knowing how to write is knowing how to ascend. Feet, arms, wings, all these are given to man by his first and most humble schoolbooks".[20] He further says that 'a school is a forge of the mind; woe to peoples without schools!'

5. *Empowerment*

The unique power of education/knowledge to contribute to personal empowerment and economic development – together to human development – has been well recognized. Robeyns has described education's contribution to personal empowerment and personal enjoyment. Education, by developing and enhancing capabilities, is a critical part of wider empowerment process through which people can exercise greater control over their lives and over their well-being. Amartya Sen focusses on human capabilities rather than on humans as a form of capital, and emphasizes the role of development in expanding personal freedoms by enhancing those capabilities and fostering an environment conducive to the functioning of those capabilities.

Education provides individuals and groups ability to form social relationships on the basis of equality with others and feel dignity and self-respect. In the human capability, framework to be illiterate and innumerate is, inter alia, to be deprived of an enabling environment for the enjoyment of a long, healthy and creative life.[21] Education of value draws out the faculties of students so as to enable them to solve the problems of life. Enabling all persons, including marginalised persons and communities to transcend poverty and obtain the means to participate fully and effectively in community life, education is instrumental in empowering them. It affords both economic levelling and social mobility in a changing world. It is in this context General Comment 13 of the International Covenant of Economic, Social and Cultural Rights, regarded education as an empowerment right.

In fact, education explicitly provides the weaker sections voice and empower them. Education and skill help people to govern their own lives. Evidence from a cross-section of countries shows the linkages between empowerment and good governance. Educated persons achieve higher score in social development which contributes to higher level of participation in social, political and economic processes which is crucial in empowerment.

Learning results in knowledge, skills and values that the learner can put to good use and attain ability to accomplish goals that were unattainable before. Knowledge and power are intimately bound together. In fact, knowledge is power.[22] There is no knowledge that is not power; and without knowledge prodigious effect of any kind can never be produced. The more one knows the more one will be able to control events.[23] Men of knowledge could increase their strength. That is, with knowledge/ education, one's potential or abilities in life will increase and such persons will truly be empowered. This is why highly successful persons seek to acquire more education and knowledge – valuable assets that serve instrumental role in their empowerment.

Education and the knowledge it provides, play a role in reinforcing or subverting established relations of power.[24] Equality in power of knowledge facilitates interaction between persons at different levels on an equal basis. Power of knowledge enables one to diagnose, and define 'a problem –socio-economic or political that needs to be addressed, and decide on his own the appropriate ways to solve them.

Basic education strengthens what individuals and communities can undertake and prepares the way for greater opportunities and choices in the next generation.[25] Educated persons and communities can easily secure their fundamental freedoms and rights, and, fight against discrimination in its various forms. They will have the potential to overcome alienation, marginalisation and powerlessness. Alienated citizens remaining passive, disengaged and withdrawn and who are found inactive in socio-political spheres would be invigorated and encouraged to be active, efficacious and involved and engaged in public sphere through education. A university can promote and encourage creative potentials of the students/groups by building self-confidence, courage and removing fear of authority and building ability to challenge a current paradigm.[26]

Education as a liberating force by itself could liberate persons who are controlled and dictated by others and bring down bossism; enhance political efficacy, civic competence and political potency. It could produce individuals who are confident, autonomous, dignified, curious, critical, constructive, creative and caring, and who will be audacious, basically optimistic despite difficulties and sufferings.[27] It could help children transform into free human beings. All these are requirements for empowerment of the individual.

Nevertheless, in spite of one's knowledge/education, if he fails to acquire the power to liberate himself from all bonds, his knowledge/education would be useless. Pursuit of professional education by the privileged sections simply for employment and making more money and acquiring status in society barely helps the community to empower itself.

6. Community Building

A strong positive relationship between community and student outcomes is hypothesised. Education 'draws or guides individuals out of themselves so that they can establish a conscious relationship with themselves and their physical and social environment."[28] Such impacts cannot help but dramatically affect the ways in which humans interact with each other and organise their social institutions. Stenhouse argues, education directly affects human relations, both in terms of individuals and groups. In fact, education has the potential to accomplish worthy ends of coalescing together different groups into a resilient and enduring community of men united to contribute to public good. It could help to promote mutual, inter-personal, inter-group, inter-community understanding, respect, cooperation, harmony, the attitude of tolerance and solidarity and peaceful coexistence, harmonious and stable relations among communities and common goals of people and the values of egalitarianism, community life and culture.

By improving himself, an educated person serves his community and country. For this educational institutions must strive to build community and a sense of community, nurture and promote supportive community/social relations, encourage cooperative human and social activity, shared values and beliefs, connections, caring, interdependence; strengthen commonalities within community relationship, recognize, reconcile and tolerate existing differences between competing values, beliefs and practices within the group of students and create confidence in terms of security of being known, of belonging to a group and of being significant, in contrast to those more contractual, hierarchical and impersonal relations[29] frequently found in some private self-financing institutions in which conservative values are perpetuated.

7. Serving as Instrument to Social Change

Education has been a powerful instrument and a key stimulus for social purposes to achieve broader socio-economic-political and cultural change since the times of ancient civilizations, despite it being used to serve the purpose of perpetuation of a privileged status quo, as the Millennium Task Force on Education has pointed out. It is used as the most powerful weapon to change societies and the world. Initiating changes in social institutions and sub-systems, education affects the social situation of a country. Educating the poor is particularly important for triggering broader social change. The Education Commission Report (Kothari Commission) emphasised that, "if we invested adequately in education, we would be able to transform society peacefully." Education Commission of 1964-66 (Dr. Radhakrishnan Commission) observed that, "for achieving change on a grand scale the only effective instrument is education." Gewirtz and Cribb emphasise that, "Education is centrally concerned with making, using and sharing the tools that enable us to understand – and change – the world."[30]

Considered as the prime agent for social transformation and the harbinger of social equality, ushering in some kind of an egalitarian society, based on justice, education can be used as a means to overcome handicaps, achieve greater equality, dignity and peace; to acquire wealth and status for all and to remove the disadvantage and bridge/eliminate the disparities between people, socio-economic groups and regions. Educational expansion narrows social inequalities by promoting a meritocratic basis for status attainment in which talented can achieve appropriate positions in the politico-administrative system, regardless of social background. Plan of Action for the United Nations Decade for Human Rights Education emphasised gender equality as one of the aims of education. Mutual trust building between citizens starts in classrooms. Schools are places for imparting the most vital of skills: tolerance, mutual respect and the ability to live peacefully with others. It is the only source through which the marginalised can be mainstreamed.

Inequalities in educational experiences and uneven educational processes are implicated in the reproduction of broader social inequalities. Hence, despite the positive impact education has on narrowing social inequalities, doubts have also been expressed on such positive relations as contained in research findings of Hannum and Buchmann as stated: "Numerous empirical studies....have indicated that while educational expansion tends to offer absolute benefits to disadvantaged groups, it is less likely to erode social inequalities rapidly, except perhaps for inequalities associated with gender, entrenched caste domination etc. Inequalities associated with economic origins or ethnicity often proves resistant to educational expansion, as educational access may expand faster for advantaged than disadvantaged groups."[31]

8. Anomic Conduct

The wrong type of education can fuel anomic reactions and even violent conduct/conflict. While education has the potential to act as a force for peace, 'educational institutions too often are used to reinforce the social divisions, intolerance and prejudices',[32] political and cultural domination, the subordination of marginalised groups and religious/ethnic divide that may lead to social conflict. Education system may also be used to foster hatred and bigotry that leads to violence and social disruptions.

9. Promotion of (national) Ideology

Education plays important role in shaping human mind and human attitudes towards politics, religion and economy, and as such can be used as force for the good by promoting socially useful beliefs and cultivate good citizenship. At the same time, schools which are centres of knowledge production may be used to reward or punish knowledge, tastes and dispositions – cultural capital. And powerful rulers may use education to legitimise and promote particular ideology.

Schooling can be used to mould (brainwash) children's views, and shape their social, economic environment. Text-book can be used as effective tool of persuasion to shape citizen's views/beliefs. The political, social and ideological orientation of an individual may be influenced by the kind of education he received. Where one party or ideological domination prevails, educational programme is designed to propagate and perpetuate official policy and party ideology, instead of plurality of ideas. Schools are used to promote one ideology named "national". By inserting lessons into the curriculum, government may use/influence educational programmes for this purpose. Students are tutored to absorb one particular idea or knowledge. Hegemonic notions about social relations are being imposed on them. As a result their thoughts are stunted, progress stifled. They have inhibitions in developing independent critical thinking, knowledge innovation or intellect. Their individual self-fulfilment is retarded. They barely develop capacity to challenge dominant and aberrant values. The *New York Times* in its editorial "False Teaching for India's Students" has commented that the Narendra Modi Government in India (2014....) uses education to promote ideology of Hindu right/Hindutva.[33] Curriculum is planned to derecognise cultural differences and force different groups to accept one value taught along with the ideology. Military regimes may use education to serve their vested interests – ideological, strategic and political – coercing students to meekly accept what they are taught without question. In such context, schools have inhibitions to emerge as centres of critical thinking. Students/youth whose education is swayed, influenced, shaped and determined by a particular ideology that tramps historical facts are likely to develop arbitrariness and bias in their views on politics, culture and religion. They are muffled to think beyond the State imposed ideas and ideologies. Curriculum slanted to one ideology helps to reproduce past understandings of the world. And they will be servile to the ideology, and inflexible in outlook towards society. In fact they will be without any empowering qualities.

10. Enhancing National Pride

Educational progress enhances national pride as well as individual and community pride. Being one component of socio-economic status, education partly shapes the personal identity of the student and plays a role as a catalyst in deepening the sense of and preserving national identity among the youth and thus furthering developmental goals. It can play a major role in creating an in-depth understanding, a deep-rooted sense of belonging and sense of pride about their identity among the young generation.

Education and Human Development

Education has been the focus of a great deal of attention in development policy at the national and international levels, because of the belief that "levels of education attainment in societies correlate strongly with a vast array of important variables in the human development process."[34] Education systems and processes are components of richly complex, broader social, and human development systems.[35] A virtuous cycle between education and broader human development can be noticed.

The purpose of education is to develop every individual to his full potential. Education helps to develop children into free human beings, promotes human resources among the community/ nation and human development, and prepares for informed citizenship. It is key to personal empowerment. According to UNESCO's Global Monitoring Report on Education for All, early childhood programmes can alter the developmental trajectory of a child. The first three years are the most crucial for brain development. The role of the early years in the formation of the human brain has been highlighted by neuro-biology and other research fields. A strong correlation has been found between early care and primary school attendance and performance.

Education enables the individual and communities to develop according to their unique needs and potentialities. The Jomtien Declaration emphasised that primary education should satisfy the basic learning needs to enable human beings to survive, to develop their full capacities, to live and work in dignity, to participate fully in development, to improve the quality of their lives and to make informed decisions.

All individuals have the human right to benefit from an education that will meet their basic learning needs—'learning to know, to do, to live together and to be', and an education that seeks to tap and develop each individual's talents, potential and personalities, so that they can 'improve their lives and transform their societies.[36]

Education and Human Capital Development

In a broader human development framework, education has both instrumental and social purpose, and is a social and economic force in its own right, representing a substantial portion of investment and employment in many localities.

A country's/community's ability to learn is a function of its stock of human capital. An analysis of research findings of over hundred empirical studies shows:

Human capital stock is central to national economic development, as better-educated citizens are more productive. The strategy of building 'human capital' (via reduction of illiteracy, morbidity and increase in life expectancy) at an early stage of development contributes to quality of life and translates into widely shared growth. Education as a form of asset contributes to human capital-to enhance the contribution of labour to the production function and thus that helps to raise the status of workers. Thus, it plays a role in breaking down labour market disadvantages.

Education and training enhancing the skills and capabilities of people enhance the quality of labour and productive potentials of individuals enabling them to earn more. Employers have propensity to reward workers with higher earnings on the basis of their education and training. Human capital has been recognised as an agent of growth. Hence learning to do has become a vital function of education, particularly higher education that usually connects formal education to the world of work.

In the modern era, the rationale for growth and mass expansion of higher education has been considered as its ability to provide a workforce for a technologically driven knowledge economy. Technology transfer requires knowledgeable managers and engineers to operate new production practices. The idea that literacy alone can solve the technological, social and economic problems has general recognition. Technologies can't be put into use without infrastructural investment in education, training, research and development. Education is valued as an individual capital good, and being an asset, possession of some qualification increases a man's earning power. For instance, training of more engineers will have a monetary value for industrial efficiency.

Education and its Socio-Economic Implications

Education presents diversity of interests for different actors in society. Nonetheless, the crucial role it plays in development of man and community of men, and in improving social relations and causing development of society is widely recognized. In the long run education influences and determines the scope and character of development of a society. Education's role and development are at the heart of present debates on sustainable human development, poverty reduction, the promotion of universal human values and tolerance, and, the challenge of new information and communication technologies. A nation's expansive plans of socio-economic progress would be complemented by a corresponding network of education. And the presence of an educated elite is considered a necessary, though not sufficient, condition of sustained socio-economic development.[37] In fact, education offers an insurance scheme for a better future for individuals and communities.

A close and long-term interaction between educational and socio-economic advancement is in operation in almost every society, although the immediate motivations that lead people to education are different. Generally, education attainment level of people has broader social and economic impacts as it serves key to promote human and socio-economic and cultural development, and, to uplift and empower the less privileged sections. Education cannot be delinked from national development or national productivity as human resource development possible with education has a multiplying effect on utilisation of all other resources. This is why the Report of the Education Commission – Kothari Commission Report-(1964-66), which still serves as the benchmark for all official policy goals and action sought to link education to the task of nation-building and development projects, and emphasised the need for relating education to productivity if the nation have to secure rapid economic development and nation-building. Emphasising that 'the destiny of India is being shaped in her classrooms' the report highlighted the role of education in determining the level of prosperity, welfare and security of people in a world based on science and technology. Only education can imbue people with the knowledge, a sense of purpose and the confidence essential for building a dynamic, vibrant and cohesive nation capable of providing its people with the resources for creating better and purposeful life, and thus provide rational environment for peaceful and harmonious development. It helps human race in their onward march towards higher objectives. High rates of education enable communities/countries to achieve high levels of growth and other dimensions of development. It is one of the important social indicators and predictors of success in employment field and improved economic status. High educational qualifications are likely to lead high employment prospects yielding high wages, to provide many private and social benefits, increased economic productivity, growth and broader socio-political change,[38] and enable individuals to gain access to other socially, economically, culturally and politically valued goods. Education – a key for modernisation - promotes a sustainable world which values knowledge and promotes a culture of peace. It equips people to harness the opportunities for individual or collective benefit. Educated men and women attain greater ability to control their own lives, especially through increased 'bargaining power'.

Economic purposes of education have acquired significance in the contemporary world. Some scholars see evolution of economic purposes of education as the single most important educational development of the 20th century. Education is often treated as an essential ingredient of socio-economic progress. Economists stress a correlation between progress in education and economic productivity, growth and development, including income distribution. A two-way relationship between education and broader demographic, economic and socio-political aspects of human development system is envisaged. World Bank report, 1994, demonstrates that investments in higher education contributed to increase in labour productivity and to higher long-term economic growth essential for poverty alleviation in many developing countries. Higher portions of the populations becoming part of the workforce (human capital development) generally produce greater economic growth, since cognitive skills of people are an important determinant of aggregate economic growth.

There is a general view that primary, and to some extent secondary education, are more effective instruments for promoting economic and social development. Dakar Declaration states that "no country can be expected to develop into a modern and open economy without a certain proportion of its work force having completed secondary education."[39] Studies have shown that many development processes are feasible only when the population achieves a relatively high level of literacy.[40] 'Literacy opens the doors to better livelihoods, improved health and expanded opportunity.'[41] An optimum level of literacy/education is a pre-requisite to accomplish a reasonable level of socio-economic advancement. Increasing literacy levels have been regarded as a prerequisite for social and economic development, and as an agent of socio-economic progress as well as a reflection of the social, cultural and economic system.[42] Development – marked by industrialisation and the emergence of knowledge economies – endowed education explicitly with an economic value by forging, direct and indirect, backward and forward, linkages between education and economy.[43]

Education is a key to national construction, the principal objective of which is to raise the standard of living of the people. Its importance to the goal of achieving this objective has been well-recognized.

The National Education Policy of 1968 emphasised the importance of effecting a radical reconstruction of education for economic and cultural development of the country, for national integration and for realising the ideal of a socialist pattern of society.

Communities and nations develop slowly or rapidly, both educationally and at economic level, relative to what those communities or nations have accomplished in education. Some countries (for example European Countries) and communities benefited from the higher level of literacy and education of their members. The economic growth of Europe proceeded by a gradual process in which jobs and skills fed into each other, facilitating adaptations of a qualified labour force as much in response to as anticipation of economic change.[44] A commitment to education was one of the fundamental things that helped the East Asian miracle of rapid economic growth and dramatic reduction in poverty. It was the active learning system in South Korea and Taiwan that stimulated the rise of in-house R&D in the 1970s and led to an extraordinary increase in numbers of patents.[45] The advancement in East Asian Tigers and China arising from their steadily rising skill intensive and technology intensive production was made possible by active education, besides industrial and technology policies. For industrial and agricultural revolutions, education moved on many fronts. The social and economic advancement of the Christian community in Kerala is attributed to the educational advancement the community members are able to accomplish. Level of human development in some oil rich West Asian countries is poor because of neglect of education for the people. Importance given to higher education brought about perceptible and impressive rise in standard of living and human development in UAE. It has been pointed out that the sustained and extra-ordinarily rapid global economic growth experienced during the post second world war period and the human demographic transition would not have been possible without the spread of mass basic and advanced education.[46]

The modern channels of mass communication, upon which a modern industrial society depends, will not function perfectly without modern education.

It is argued and shown that within societies, expansion of educational opportunities enables individuals to improve their economic circumstances.[47] Studies by researchers have found that at micro level individuals who have more education earn more.[48] Empirical studies support the proposition that greater education attainment and/or education expenditure contributes to higher economic growth.[49] In fact, the economy is one of the potentially most direct beneficiaries of education development. That education, one of the few sure roads to economic progress, has become a contemporary creed.[50] Higher GDP and GDP per capita is achieved because of higher education.

Education and Non-Economic Implications

Notwithstanding its economic advantages education has non-economic impacts too. It plays a key role in social development objectives to achieve inclusive growth, social cohesion and accountability in development. Amartya Sen emphasised education as an important parameter for any inclusive growth in an economy. It is important to provide equity and opportunity, and a voice to those who have been excluded, to provide gender equality and social equality. It is rightly stated that, "education beyond all other devices of human origin, is the greatest equaliser of the conditions of men, the balance wheel of the social machinery. Values inculcated in schools can make children less susceptible to the kind of prejudices, bigotry, extreme nationalism, racism and lack of tolerance."[51]

Ignorance and immorality of sections of people could only be overcome through the redemptive powers of the schools.[52] When a large number of the members of socially and educationally backward classes get educated better and represented in the legislatures, public employment, professions and participate in other walks of public life, the attitude that they are inferior will disappear. This will promote fraternity; assure the dignity of the individual and the unity and integrity of the nation. An egalitarian society will be the outcome of this process.

Education – an indispensable asset of every individual and community and every nation – can accelerate the pace towards a better and higher quality of life and enhance self-confidence and competences required to perform a task effectively and to interact with people proficiently. Increase of social wealth and improvement of social relations take place on the basis of development of man which can be attained through educational programmes.[53] Bhatnagar's study shows that 'a large number of better educated persons irrespective of their low or high caste categories have higher attitude scores on family, religion, marriage and education.'[54] Education and the economic well-being of an individual give him/her a status in society and increase his/her self-esteem and dignity. Education is a means to claim the ladder of socio-economic status in society. For example, a greater number of persons belonging to higher status communities/castes such as the Christians, Nairs, Namboothiris, Brahmins, etc. are more educated as compared to lower status groups like Muslims, scheduled caste/tribes.

Countries with better educated citizens are likely to have healthier, slower growing populations, as educated individuals make better health choices, live longer, and may have healthier and fewer children. Education contributes to improve child and maternal health.

The 2011 Global Monitoring Report provides striking new evidence on the health benefits associated with maternal education. Using household survey data it shows that, in many countries mothers who are more educated are more likely to choose better preventive measures. Evidence from household surveys consistently points to maternal education as one of the strongest factors influencing children's prospects of survival.[55]

Education has great significance in specific contexts and difficult circumstances of political violence, communal/caste riots, group rivalries, civil unrest, armed conflicts, human displacements etc. And a world of peace, dignity, justice and equality depends on many factors; education is central among them. The preamble to the constitution of UNESCO states "...the wide diffusion of culture, and the education of humanity for justice and liberty and peace are indispensable to the dignity of man."

Education and Governance Quality

More educated and healthier young people provide greater social stability. Countries with more educated populations are likely to be more democratic, as their citizens are able to make more informed political decisions.[56] Well-educated individuals are placed by society for the maintenance of a stable democracy.[57]

Poorly educated persons would neither govern nor be easily governed, and they cannot be good statesmen, or lawyers, or doctors, or artisans, or mechanics, or farmers and they make very poor labourers, and worse citizens.[58] To manage a state/society and for a well-developed economy, enough trained and competent people as well as improvement in the general, technical and cultural standard of the working people are needed. Then a community can be confident about its future.

Negative Effects of Education

While education is generally perceived as a good thing in various ways for people who are differently located, and its effects on individuals and society are of high value, it is also "connected more widely with power and social inequality".[59] Education system may be used to transmit the ignorance, prejudice and social injustice that make societies less cohesive, more divided and more likely to descend into unrest and violence.[60] Under wrong conditions education can push communities to conflicts. The wrong type of education can reinforce social divisions, foster hostility between groups. Grievances over education may reinforce wider social, economic and political grievances. Different school systems may tend to reinforce mutually hostile mindsets and identities. Schools may be used to foment violence, although they have the potential to calm disturbed minds. It is an irony that Lant Pritchett found no relationship between rising education attainment and growth.[61]

Consequences of Lack of Education

Individuals/communities/countries with less education find themselves at drawbacks and deprivations relative to those with more. Community disadvantage and inequalities in education and employment differently reflect in the life chances of individuals.

For those who are deprived of education, many individual rights, especially rights associated with employment and social security, are beyond their reach. Uneducated or poorly educated children are often found thrown into the streets and market places, end up in undesirable groups which disorient them to extreme conduct, "become drunkards, thieves, pickpockets, incendiaries, terrorists or leaders of the mob (a dangerous class) and finally die in the gutter, the almshouse or the prison."[62] Their life will be defined by ignorance and immorality. Children would become 'discontented, useless, and bad citizens' without systematic school education. Ignorant and poor people, out of their frustration, tend to commit crimes that destroy peace, prosperity and happiness of society. Only by availing equal opportunities to all, this situation can be avoided, and the power of schools in solving such social problems has been widely recognised. When poverty leads to criminality, schools could cure both maladies. Well-educated individuals may make better citizens, although it is not a rule.

Conclusion

The education system in a plural society of diversities and disparities, and consisting people at different levels of development seeks to ensure all-round development of humans. It seeks to enhance and develop individual's capabilities so that they become confident, autonomous, free, creative, constructive and optimistic. The educated acquire power to liberate themselves from all bonds, and take control of their own destiny. Education, by developing and enhancing capabilities, is a critical part of wider empowerment process through which people can exercise greater control over their lives and over their well-being.

The importance of education in socio-economic advancement of communities notwithstanding, a hierarchy of education in which different groups of people with different levels of economic status gets different types of education may promote unequal development in society. If the differently educated reinforce status values and special privileges that are incompatible with socio-economic advance, societal development will be affected. The need for a proper, equitable accessible education system is obvious here. It also highlights the need to avoid wasteful and dysfunctional investment in education.

Notes and References

1. *Oxford Advanced Learner's Dictionary*, 2010.
2. Alan Macfarlane (2009), 'Reflections on Cambridge', Social Science Press: New Delhi, p. 187.
3. Quoted in Mohd. Sharif Khan (2002), 'Education, Religion and Modern Age', APH Publishing Corporation, New Delhi, p. 31.
4. *Ibid.*, Mohd. Sharif Khan, p. 21.
5. Letter to Manilal Gandhi, 12 October, 1909 (CW 9, P 475).
6. *Harijan*, 23 May, 1936.
7. *Harijan*, 19 January, 1947, p. 494.
8. World Bank, 1994, p. 1.
9. en.wikipedia.org/wik/education
10. Tariq Ramadan (2010), *The Quest for Meaning: Developing a Philosophy of Pluralism*, Penguin, London.
11. Jose Marti (2009), *On Education*, edited by Philip S. Foner, Aakar Books, New Delhi, p. 79.
12. Alan Macfarlane (2009), *Reflections on Cambridge*, Social Science Press, New Delhi, p. 187.

13. *Education for All Global Monitoring Report*, 2011, UNESCO Publishing, p. 174.
14. Talcot Parsons (1961), The school class as a social system, in AH Halsey, J. Floudand CA Anderson, (Eds.) *Education, Economy and Society: a reader in the sociology of education*, Free Press, New York, p. 440. Also quoted in Sharon Gewirtz and Alan Cribb (2009), *Understanding Education: A Sociological Perspective*, Polity Press, Cambridge, pp. 28-29.
15. S. Bowles and H. Gintis (1988), Reply to our critics, in M. Cole (ed.), *Bowles and Gintis revisited: Correspondence and contradiction in educational theory*, Falmer Press, London and New York, p. 235.
16. *See* Janet R. Dickson *et al.*, (Eds.) (2010), *Advancing Global Education; Patterns of Potential Human Progress*, Vol. 2, Oxford, New Delhi, p. 155.
17. John C., Caldwell (1980), Mass Education as a determinant of the timing of fertility decline, *Population and Development Review* 6 (2), June, pp. 225-255.
18. Jose Marti (2009), *On Education*, edited by Philip S. Foner, Aakar Books, New Delhi, p. 24.
19. Alan Macfarlane (2009), *Reflections on Cambridge*, Social Science Press, New Delhi, p. 190.
20. Jose Marti, *Ibid.*, pp. 26-68.
21. Janet R. Dickson, p. 13.
22. First stated by Imam Ali (599–661 CE) the first Imam of Shia community.
23. Francis Bacon (2005), *The American Heritage, New Dictionary of Cultural Literacy*, Third Edition, Houghton Mifflin Company.
24. Sharon Gewirtitz and Alan Cribb (2009), '*Understanding Education*', Polity Press, Cambridge, p. 7.
25. www.unesco.edu
26. Alan Macfarlane (2009), *Reflections on Cambridge*, Social Science Press, New Delhi, p. 198.
27. Tariq Ramadan (2010), *op cit.*, p. 131.
28. *Ibid.*, p. 127.
29. To know more about the idea of community, see Patricia Colderwood (2000), *Learning Community: Finding Common Ground in Difference*, Teachers College, Columbia University, New York.
30. Sharon Gewirtz and Alan Cribb (2009), *Understanding Education: A Sociological Perspective*, Polity Press, Cambridge, pp. 9-10.
31. Emily Hannum and Claudia Buchanan (2006), 'Global Education Expansion and Socio-Economic Development: An Assessment of Findings from the Social Sciences', in Joel E. Cohen *et al.*, (Eds.), 'Educating All Children: A Global Agenda', Cambridge, MA, American Academy of Arts and Sciences, pp. 495-534. Also see Janet

R. Dickson *et al.*, (2010), Advancing Global Education; Patterns of Potential Human Progress', Vol. 2, Oxford, New Delhi, p. 15.

32. *See Education for All Global Monitoring Report,* 2011 UNESCO Report, 2011 UNESCO Publishing, Highlights, p. 3.
33. timesofindia.indiatimes/India/Modis-educational-reform NYTservice/october9.2014promote-ideology of Hinduright-NYT/articles/44742331.com
34. Janet R. Dickson *et al.*, (eds.), *op cit.*, p. 159.
35. Tariq Ramadan (2010), *op cit.*, p. 7.
36. 'Education for All: Meeting Our Collective Commitments', Text adopted by the World Education Forum, Dakar, Senegal, April 26-28, 2000.
37. *Ibid.*, p. 277.
38. *Op cit.*, Janet R. Dickson (2010), p. 166.
39. UNESCO 2000:16.
40. Katarina Schuth (1980), 'Village Literacy and its Correlates: A Mysore Case Study, In An Exploration of India Geographical Perspectives on Society and Culture', ed. David E Sopher, Ithaca, New York: Cornell University Press, pp. 191-212.
41. *Education for All Global Monitoring Report,* 2011, UNESC Publishing, Highlights, p. 7.
42. Government of India, Education Commission Report, 1966; also Moonis Raza (1990), *'Education, Development and Society'*, New Delhi, Vikas Publishing House.
43. *See* Pawan Agarwal (2009), *Indian Higher Education: Envisioning the Future,* Sage, New Delhi, p. 169.
44. *Ibid.*, p. 251.
45. *Innovation and Development,* Routledge, Taylor and Francis Group, Vol. 1, Number 1, April 2011, p. 21.
46. Janet R. Dickson (2010), *op cit.*, p. 155.
47. *See* Janet R. Dickson *et al.*, (2010), p. 15.
48. *Ibid.*, p. 143.
49. Steven. N., Durlauf *et al.*, *Growth Econometrics;* In Philippe Aghion and Steven N. Durlauf, (Eds.), Handbook of Economic Growth, Vol. 1A, Amsterdam Elsvier, 2005, pp. 555-677.
50. Mary Jean Brown, C. Arnold Anderson (1971), *Concerning the Role of Education in Development,* in Clifford Geertz (ed.) *Old Societies and New States, The Quest for Modernity in Asia and Africa,* Amerind Publishing Co. Pvt. Ltd., New Delhi, p. 247.
51. *Education for All Global Monitoring Report,* UNESCO Publishing, 2011, p. 167.
52. William J. Reese (2002), *'Power and the Promise of School Reform'*, Teachers College Press, Columbia University, New York and London, p. 10.

53. M.S. Gore, *et al.*, (Eds.) (1990) *Social Implications of Development: The Asian Experience*, Indian Academy of Social Science, Vidhya Prakash, Private Ltd, Allahabad.
54. Bhatnagar, G.S. (1972), *Education and Social Change*, Minerva Associates, Calcutta.
55. For details, see *Education for All Global Monitoring Report*, 2011, Highlights, p. 5.
56. See Janet R. Dickson *et al.*, (2010), p. 15, *op cit.*
57. Peter Self (1972), *Administrative Theories and Politics*, George Allen and Unwin Ltd, London, p. 268.
58. *Rochester School Report*, 1845, 25, quoted in William J. Reese, *op cit.*, p. 13.
59. Sharon Gewirtz and Alan Cribb (2009), *op cit.*, p. 4.
60. *Education for All Global Monitoring Report*, 2011, UNESCO Publishing, p. 134.
61. Lant Pritchett (1996), *Where has all the Education Gone*? World Bank Policy Research Working Paper Series No. 1581, World Bank, Washington DC.
62. David B. Tyack, *The Spread of Public Schooling in Victorian Froerica*, 1978:174, quoted in William J. Reese, *op cit.*, p. 10.

3

Empowerment: The Concept and Dimensions—Theoretical Perspectives

The concept of empowerment is used in a variety of senses and in different contexts; and perceptions of being empowered vary across time, culture, and domains of personal life. Some social scientists consider the concept as a part of globalisation and structural adjustment programmes of western capitalism for which empowerment of the marginalised sections of the society seeks only an institutionalised mode of giving power to them.

In fact, empowerment is multidimensional, and has sociological, psychological, economic, political and cultural dimensions. It occurs at individual, group, community and national level. In the sociological context, it is used to entail ending of social discrimination of members of groups or communities on the grounds of caste, religion, race, ethnicity, colour or gender, and enabling them to attain resources to overcome these discriminations and to participate in the making of socio-economic and political decisions that affect their life. Empowerment of the powerless depends on their liberation from subordination, inequality, and inequity. This essentially involves a process of inclusion in social life against exclusion.

In its psychological dimension, empowerment assumes an emotional state characterised by individual's feelings of competence, meaningfulness, and choice that impact his works. In economic sense, to empower the poor, they need be provided with greater economic power to serve their wants and change their social constructions. For R. Kenneth Godwin for whom citizen empowerment is like consumer sovereignty,[1] empowering policies mean limiting government and providing the poor with greater economic power to serve their wants and change their social constructions.

Empowering involves developing one's potential, enhancing his productivity and creativity in his work and developing strong and positive relationship with other members of the community and contributing to them. It requires strengthening people's capacities. Individuals and communities need be strengthened with increased spiritual, political, social, educational and economic power. People need to acquire ability to organise themselves for mutual help and increase their own self-reliance. In this sense, empowerment of the disadvantaged sections of the population focuses on mobilizing their self-help efforts, rather than providing them with social welfare which will keep them dependent on charity – a disempowering phenomenon. Ability to exercise choices in and control over their lives is critical. Empowered people have freedom of choice and action. This in turn enables them to better influence the course of their lives and the decisions which affect them. In essence empowerment involves self-determined change. One must have capacity to influence the direction of change and ability to gain control over resources. In fact, individual empowerment takes place in a variety of circumstances and conditions. In this context, it is desirable that a theory of empowerment must be contextual, interdisciplinary and multi-dimensional.

World Bank defines empowerment as a process of enhancing the capacity of individuals or groups to make purposive choices and to transform them in to desired actions and outcomes. For this to materialise, it is central to build individual and collective assets, and improve the efficiency and fairness of organisational and institutional contexts which govern the core of these assets.[2] Expansion of assets and capability of poor people help them to participate, negotiate with, influence, control, and hold accountable institutions that affect their lives. The level of one's capacity to realise whatever he/she feels is necessary for his/her well-being, and the skills and means necessary for realising one's purposes, determines his/her empowerment. People must be able to undertake the task of restructuring the conditions of their living so as to liberate themselves from hopelessness, passivity, dejection and depression.[3]

Empowerment and Exercise of Power

In a realistic sense, empowerment is referred to imply the "process by which individuals and groups gain power (social and political), access to resources and control over their own lives, destiny and environment, and thus gain the ability to achieve their highest personal and collective aspirations and goals."[4] One also gains influence over others, institutions and society. In fact, empowerment promotes individual's/community's ability to control and to effect change in the environment. Empowerment of the weaker sections implies their shaping and sharing of power – equally and freely – with other sections and enjoying dignity and privileges as others have in political, economic, social and cultural affairs. An empowered individual will have the ability to achieve transition from a state of powerlessness and helplessness to a state of relative control over his life, destiny and environment and develop confidence in his own capacities. Development of abilities is the main means of emerging from situations of powerlessness, despite the fact that powerless people suffer from lack of resources.

People's belief in their own ability to achieve outcomes is an achievement in terms of a sense of individual ability to control one's life.[5] Exercise of power is primarily an action oriented to achieve strategic advantages in social relations. The problem of empowerment is how to activate power in an individual in order to influence the power field, in a way that bring more control in their lives.[6]

Empowerment is compared to a circular process of social change and activation of abilities and resources, in which human agents in need of empowerment, act together with empowering human agents.[7] It has to deal explicitly with problems of powerlessness fostered by numerous factors, including structures and systems. Empowered individuals/groups/communities are able to fully access personal/collective power, authority and influence, and to employ that strength positively when engaging with other people, institutions or society and feel hopeful, active, satisfied and cheerful.

By Bush and Folger's definition, "*empowerment* means the restoration to individuals of a sense of their own value and strength and their own capacity to handle life's problems."[8] In their treatment, empowerment does not include 'power balancing' or redistribution of power in order to protect weaker persons;" nor does it mean redistributing resources or power from stronger to weaker persons. It cannot be the giving of power by the powerful to the powerless which will only disempower the powerful. "Empowerment is not giving people power; people already have plenty of power, in the wealth of their knowledge and motivation, to do their jobs magnificently."[9] Empowerment is letting this power out.[10] It requires sharing powers with all, not to impose or convey. And one needs to be helped to build one's own power base. For this, civil and political rights are to be guaranteed to enable people to shape public life as well as their private lives which make human empowerment possible.

Empowerment and Leadership

Empowerment encourages people to gain the skills and knowledge to overcome obstacles in life, in work environment or within themselves or in the society. A group that is in the process of empowering itself develops its own leadership. One's leadership and decision-making opportunity and ability have a bearing on his/her empowerment. In a broader sense, empowerment has been defined as character education and leadership development.[11]

The contextual theory of empowerment presents the transition from powerlessness to more control in life as a change in both human activity and the social structure. The essence of empowerment was expressed by Elanor Roosevelt when he said, "We must do that which we think we cannot."[12] The realization of people's aspirations depends on abilities and resources which enable organized activity.

Community Empowerment

Disempowerment of members of a particular community renders them powerless which influences their lives, futures and fate. Empowerment theory diagnoses powerlessness as a social problem and not an individual problem. The power relations and the disempowering socio-political practices create powerlessness among the people.

Powerlessness and helplessness result in loss of control. A powerless and disempowered community is systematically denied identities and roles possessing social values, and important resources.[13] These roles and resources are considered as the basis for the exertion of interpersonal influence and for effective social functioning. Hence, inability to exert interpersonal influence and inability to function effectively in society are structural manifestations of powerlessness which can be overcome with empowerment of the community.

Powerless people lack self-worth, and are in a condition of self-blame, indifference towards, and alienation from the environment, beside inability to act for themselves, and of growing dependence on social services and specialists/experts for the solution of their problems.[14]

Empowerment, conceived as a process centred in local community, involves mutual respect, critical reflection, caring and group participation, through which people lacking an equal share of valued resources, gain greater access to and control over these resources.[15] Community empowerment entails a collective social process of organising and creating a community and the community achieving better control over the environment and participates in decision-making, and gains self-esteem, self-efficacy, competency and locus of control. Disenfranchised social groups aspiring empowerment work to change their social surroundings, change detrimental policies and structures, and work to fulfil their needs.[16] The oppressed, being liberated, and being active participants and managers of their own affairs, may gain empowerment.

People as community gain real and concrete power over the institutions which control their everyday lives. The community that suffers from social stigma and discrimination acquires ability to control its relevant environment better and to influence its future and develops a sense of responsibility, commitment and ability to care for collective survival, as well as skills in problem-solving, and political efficacy to influence changes in environment that impinge on their quality of life.[17] Collective action to access government and other community resources are its key elements.

Regarding empowerment, a connection between the individual and the community is envisaged. The abilities acquired by the individuals contribute to the joint goals of empowering themselves as individuals and as a community.[18] People help people to attain personal growth through community empowerment.[19] Individual empowerment is presumed to create a community potential. Self-efficacy may become collective efficacy if it gets translated into the community's practical ability to organise itself for a collective effort to achieve outcomes in the environment. Individual empowerment creates a reservoir of community potential that helps to realise community empowerment. In this process the individuals and communities increase their spiritual, political, social and economic strength. It is a transition from a passive situation to a more active situation of control. This depends on the community's acquisition of ability and access to essential resources. A community's access to necessary resources determines/enhances its ability to act and to influence. A community deprived of access to these resources will have little ability to influence the social structure or to influence the creation of rules and laws. Empowerment, then, begins with people's/community's will to obtain resources and means to develop ability in order to achieve something in their lives.

Powerlessness of an individual changes by means of his activism in collaboration with others in his own situation in a social environment free of inequalities. This process empowers the entire community of men, although individual empowerment need not always result in community empowerment.

Social structure conditions the process of empowerment. The individual through his power of empowerment creates expectations for change on the social structure level. Community empowerment takes place when these expectations begin to materialise.[20] Personal efficacy draws its strength from structural forms of control that are embedded in social systems.[21] Hence, the empowerment process depends on what already exists in the society, but the success of the process is defined by what and how much changes on the personal level, the community level, and the social systems connected with the process.[22]

The potential for community empowerment exists in every environment, just as the potential for individual empowerment exists in every person. In every process of individual empowerment, there also exists a potential for community empowerment, and every process of community empowerment creates an environment that facilitates individual empowerment.[23]

Community empowerment contributes to individual empowerment. Collective decision-making and shared leadership are important elements in community empowerment.

A community's active involvement in civic and social life and engagement with the state and the rulers to negotiate for their rights is in proportion to its empowerment. A community/group must make and own its decisions, so that its members can develop and experience their own power.[24] Empowerment enables the community to make their own decisions regarding their life situations and self-manage the tasks and issues they face. Empowerment of community improves its perceived as well as the actual ability to control social processes. Members of the community attain self-confidence and resilience when faced with setbacks, and the ability to visualize themselves overcoming problems. As the community moves to a higher level of empowerment, it no longer needs the professional services that were essential in the stages of transition from powerlessness and hence its dependence on professionals/bureaucrats gets lessened.

Marginalised people/communities who are excluded from social processes and restricted from access to socio-economic and political opportunities can be empowered by providing them basic opportunities to achieve self-sufficiency. They need encouragement and development of skills for their self-sufficiency and self-reliance. Their empowerment is dependent on their ability to make decisions that affect their lives, order their private life as they choose. A programme for their empowerment requires removal of the disabilities which they suffer from. Conditions that foster powerlessness in life situations need be identified and removed. Empowerment as a personal process and community process being connected has influence on powerless people.

Empowerment, in short, essentially requires capabilities like the ability to make decisions about personal/collective circumstances, to access information and resources for decision-making, to consider a range of options from which to choose (freedom of choice), to exercise assertiveness in collective decision-making, to have confidence about the ability to make change, to learn and access skills for improving personal/collective circumstances involved in the growth process and changes self-initiation, increase one's positive self-image and overcome stigma, etc.[25]

Some of the elements considered crucial to empowerment are a sense of self-worth and dignity by the people; the ability of the people to determine their life affairs autonomously and independent of any interference and free from any dependence; access to and control and influence over resources; attain mobility and social interaction and a collective sense and solidarity among groups.

Strategies of Empowerment

Empowerment of citizens, individually or as communities, depends on their abilities to overcome problems through their own initiatives'.[26] Complete enjoyment of socio-economic and cultural right is essential. They need to have participation in socio-economic spheres. Fawcett identifies four strategies for promoting community empowerment viz. enhancing experience and competence, enhancing group structure in capacity, removing social and environment barriers and enhancing environment support and resources.[27] Individual and community disabilities also need to be removed. A programme to make the people self-sufficient enabling them to self-support, ending dependency is necessary. Education, health-care, governance, economic policies and activities – all seek to empower people by increasing development opportunities, enhancing development outcomes and improving people's quality of life. Education, organization and networking are suggested as strategies for empowering disenfranchised and oppressed people.

Empowerment through Education

Education is a contested domain – one in which there are many disputes about its purposes and its various effects on individuals and societies. Nonetheless, considered generally as a good thing, education is considered as a critical part of wider empowerment process through which people can exercise greater control over their lives and over the well-being of their family members. Education/knowledge is also connected more widely with power.[28] Imam Ali (599–661 CE), the first Imam of Shia Muslims stated "knowledge is power". The more one knows/educates, the more one will be able to control events.[29] There is no knowledge that is not power and without knowledge no great effects of any kind can be produced. Only men of knowledge could increase their strength. That is, with education/knowledge one's potential or abilities in life increases and such persons get empowered. Perhaps, this is the motivation for men's desires to acquire more knowledge about their fields of activity. For them, knowledge that helps to analyse the complex problems they face, is instrumental in their empowerment. In fact, educational power of people is key to their empowerment. Education and related social conditions would enable persons to gain empowerment. The less privileged, oppressed and exploited people need to be liberated through education in order to enable them to empower. Education and related social conditions would enable persons to gain empowerment. Being able to chart a course of their own to fulfill their needs, educated persons empower themselves by taking responsibility for their own and the community's progress. They can effectively participate in developing policies and institutions/ structures appropriate to meet their needs and strategies for realising those policies. They act on their own purposes, values, feelings and meanings rather than on those which they have uncritically assimilated from others in order to gain greater control over their life as socially responsible, clear thinking decision-makers.[30] They develop ability to challenge entrenched wrong assumptions and strength to resolve intractable conflicts in the community/society. Education need to be oriented to nurture these qualities. Educational efforts must include strategies to meet the needs of the less powerful and the disenfranchised groups.

The education system that denies access to the disadvantaged sections in the society adversely affects their empowerment. Inequality in distribution of educational resources, education success, employment opportunities and income is a distorting factor in empowerment of the disadvantaged sections.

Empowerment through Organisation

For poor, marginalized people who are not able to express their voice, organisation provides them with a forum to express their community needs which cannot be easily ignored. As Alinsky opines, "Building a strong, lasting and staffed organisation alters the relations of power. Once such an organisation exists, people on the 'other side' must always consider the organisation when making decisions".[31] By organizing the community, power is bulid up in a step by step approach.

Networking with others also helps members of disenfranchised communities to realize and extend power. Structured networking can be used as an empowerment tool. It can provide for social interaction with goodwill toward others regardless of caste, race, gender, creed or religion, and help diverse groups share political, social and economic power.

Empowering Minority Communities

Empowerment is crucial for progress of weaker sections, especially minorities in any society. Only through empowerment can they be liberated from structures of exploitation, oppression, discrimination, subordination, dependence, servitude etc. The welfare, social justice and empowerment of the minorities who are disadvantaged, powerless and marginalised must be sought to be achieved by bringing them into the mainstream of development by making them self-reliant. A programme for their integration into the social, political, economic and cultural process is necessary to empower them. This can be secured through education and economic and political measures. Minorities, particularly the Muslim community, need to be educationally empowered and enabled to receive equal opportunities, equal access and privileges in all areas of life.

Issues in Empowerment of Minorities

It is pointed out that students from dominated societal groups are either empowered or disabled as a direct result of their interactions with educators in schools[32] and that human relationships are at the heart of schooling.[33] That "the relationship between the majority and the minority is inseparably intertwined with value differentials, with minority on the losing side"[34] is reflected in cases of Muslim boys and girls who strictly observe Islamic customs and practices encountering pressure and hostile attitude from fellow and teacher members in numerous non-Muslim schools. This affects their desire to assimilate into the mainstream society. This situation tends to damage their mental health and self-esteem. The outcome of such pressure causes heightened anxiety, lower self-esteem, feeling of marginality and identity[35], confusion, especially in children attributing their disadvantaged position to some fault in themselves. That is, those students are put in a position to degrade themselves. As Cummins observes, "Subordinated group members often partially internalise the ways they are defined or positioned by the dominant group and come to see themselves as inferiors".[36]

Minority Muslim students attending schools run by majority community management or overwhelmingly dominated by prejudiced and hostile majority are sometimes constrained to depend on or to conform to the norms of the ongoing majority. This subordination of the Muslim community students tends to develop negative concept of them and makes their involvement/ engagement in collective efforts difficult. Since power relationship between the minority and majority is at the heart of empowerment process, empowerment of minorities in this uncomfortable relation is also hindered. The minority who strives for their empowerment must be believed, recognised, respected, cared, listened, obeyed and distinguished by others.

Notes and References

1. Helen Ingram and Steven Rathgeb Smith (Eds.) (1995), *Public Policy for* Democracy, Frank Brothers and Co., Massachuset Avenue, p. 159.
2. www.worldbank.org
3. *See* Ramashray Roy (1999), *'Dalits, Development and Democracy'*, Shipra, New Delhi, p. 148.
4. Robbins, Chattergee and Canda (1998), visit www.malone.edu/media; www.mpow.org
5. Bandura (1997), *Developing a Theory of Empowerment*, p. 152.
6. Visit http://www.beyondintractability.org/essay/empowerment, p. 164.
7. *Ibid.*, p. 149.
8. Robert A. Baruch Bush and Joseph P. Folger (1994), *'The Promise of Mediation: Responding to Conflict Through Empowerment and Recognition'*, San Francisco: Jossey Bass Publishers, p. 2, quoted in Maire A. Dugan, Empowerment, http://www.beyondintractability.org/essay/empowerment.
9. Wikipedia.

10. Kenneth H. Blanchard *et al.*, (1996), '*Empowerment Takes More than a Minute*', San Francisco: Berrett-Koehler.
11. *Wingspan Youth Development Service,* quoted in Maire Dugan (Ibid).
12. *Ibid., Wingspan Youth Empowerment Service,* http://www.wingspanyes.org.
13. Solomon (1976, 1985), in *Developing a Theory of Empowerment,* p. 153.
14. Perkins, Douglas. D, Marc A. Zimmerman (1995), Empowerment Theory, Research and Application, *American Journal of Community Psychology,* Vol. 23, Number 5, p. 144.
15. Cornell Empowerment Group, 1989, Empowerment and Family Support, *Networking Bulletin,* 1 (2), pp. 1-23.
16. Maire A. Dugan, *Ibid.*
17. *Ibid.*, p. 145.
18. *Developing a Theory of Empowerment,* p. 148.
19. See African-American community Empowerment Inc., (ACE) of Morris County; available at http://www.aceofmorris.org/
20. *See Developing a Theory of Empowerment,* pp. 146-147.
21. Clegg (1989), quoted in *Theories of Empowerment,* p. 150.
22. *Theories of Empowerment,* p. 150.
23. Maton and Rappaport (1984), quoted in *Developing a Theory of Empowerment,* p. 151.
24. Perkins, Douglas D., Marc A. Zimmerman (1995), Empowerment Theory, Research and Application, *American Journal of Community Psychology,* Vol. 23, Number 5, p. 145.
26. *See* Stanford Borins (1998), '*Innovating With Integrity: How Local Heroes are Transforming American Government*', George Town University Press: Washington DC; quoted in Amita Singh (2005), 'Administrative Reforms: Towards Sustainable Practices', Sage Publications, p. 120.
27. Perkins, Douglas D., Marc A. Zimmerman (1995), Empowerment Theory, Research and Application, *American Journal of Community Psychology,* Vol. 23, Number 5, p. 575.
28. Sharon Gewitz and Alan Cribb (2009), '*Understanding Education: A Sociological Perspective*', Polity Press, Cambridge, p. 41.
29. Francis Bacon (2005), *The American Heritage, New Dictionary of Cultural Literacy,* Third Edition, Houghton Miflin.
30. Visit http://www.beyondintractability.org/essay/empowerment/
31. *Ibid.*, p. 3.
32. Jim Cummins (1993), *"Empowering Minority Students: A Framework for Intervention"*, In Beyond Silenced Voices: Class, Race and Gender in the United States Schools, comp. and ed. L. Weis and M. Fine, New York: SUNY Press, pp. 101-139.
33. J. Cummins (1996), *Negotiating Identities: Education for Empowerment in a Diverse Society,* Ontario, CA: California Association for Bilingual Education, p. 12.

34. Karmela Liebkind (1989), The Identity of a Minority, *Journal of Multilingual and Multicultural Development*, Vol. 10, No.1, pp. 47-57, 53.
35. Karmela Liebkind points out "Identity relates to desire: The desire for recognition, the desire for affiliation, and the desire for security and safety"; see K. Liebkind (1989), The Identity of a Minority, *Journal of Multilingual and Multicultural Development*, Vol.10, No.1, pp. 47-57, 53.
36. J. Cummins (1996), *'Negotiating Identities: Education for Empowerment in a Diverse Society'*, Ontario, CA: California Association for Bilingual Education, p. 12.

4

Education Policy of Kerala

In this age of development, the great and all important subject of educating the entire population, the masses, cannot be neglected. The idea of mass education has been an assumed goal of state policy in almost all countries. The state has to play a powerful role in this respect, particularly in educating the poor, ignorant and disadvantageous children. Primary responsibility to provide education lies with the state. And almost everywhere government has been the principal provider of education with the objective of equipping the young generation with the necessary skills they need to escape poverty and unemployment. The rationale for public support of universal basic education has been human development and preparation for informed citizenship. Hence education has been a core aspect in development policies of nations. To promote the use of this service and to acknowledge its characteristics as merit goods, government is obliged to offer education at little or no cost to learners. To ensure not merely right of education but also free and accessible education to all segments of population is part of the state's responsibility in order to ensure conditions for decent and dignified living to its citizens.

It is the responsibility of every democratic government to encompass equal social conditions (education is a core social condition), which is best for society, in the delivery of social goods – education, health care, housing etc. that will stimulate economic activity and job creation. The state cannot disengage from this crucial role. This social role calls for active intervention of the government through positive measures to guarantee citizens the conditions to obtain proper and adequate education. It is pointed out that the objective of promoting a national ideology through state-run schools may also explain why governments provide education directly rather than subsidise families to allow children to attend private schools and why they enforce compulsory education laws.[1]

States also prefer massive expansion of education provision when consolidating political power and forging national identity. It is necessary for a multi-religious/plural society to develop an education system that promotes common good and enables the citizens to understand each other better and live in peace and harmony. The human right to benefit from an education that meets individuals' basic learning needs – learning to know, to do, to live together and to be – has been universally recognized. Such right seeks to tap and develop each individual's talents, potential and personalities, so that they can 'improve their lives and transform their societies'.[2] Hence, emphasis on increasing participation of all in education has been part of the policy of governments. Governments need to demonstrate a sense of resolve, commitment and purpose to promote a rational system of public education to benefit all sections of the society with equity, fairness and social justice.

Nonetheless, the role of the state, in the neoliberal dispensation, has changed from one of being the provider of social goods and educational facilities and the principal vehicle of socio-economic development to one of guiding and facilitating them.

Global Context in Respect of Provision of Education

Since 1952, especially when the European Convention on Human Rights obliged all signatory parties to guarantee the right to education, a pillar of which is constituted by provision of educational facilities, right to education has been recognised as a basic human right globally. Various international agreements and instruments recognize this right. The UN Declaration of Human Rights articulates access to some basic level of education as a global right of all people. Under Article 26 of the Declaration 'Everyone has the right to education. Education shall be free, at least on the elementary and fundamental stages.'

Similarly, Article 13 of the UN's International Covenant on Economic and Social and Cultural Rights of 1966 also guarantees and envisages to promote this right. ICESCR obligates states to adopt plan of action for the progressive implementation of free and compulsory education, especially, primary education for all. The ICESCR insisted to ensure higher education largely available and equally accessible to all and to achieve progressive introduction of free education at the level of higher education, recognizing parents' right to choose the kind of education they want to give their children.

The declaration adopted by the first world conference on Education for All, 1990, affirmed global education goals with respect to basic education. UNESCO formally proclaimed universal primary education as a global goal, thus promoting it to a position of global prominence. It works for promoting education as a fundamental right and for full and equal opportunities for education for all.

The project of 'Education for All' that UNESCO leads (The Dakar Framework for Action on Education for All, under the auspices of the World Education Forum, adopted in Senegal-2000) aimed to meet the learning needs of all children, youth and adults by 2015. It envisaged six goals:

1. To expand and improve comprehensive early childhood care and education, especially for the most vulnerable and disadvantaged children.
2. Ensure that by 2015, all children, particularly girls, children in difficult circumstances and those belonging to ethnic minorities, have access to complete, free and compulsory primary education of good quality.
3. Ensure that the learning needs of all young people and adults are met through equitable access to appropriate learning and life-skill programmes.
4. Achieve a 50 per cent improvement in levels of adult literacy by 2015, especially for women, and equitable access to basic and continuing education for all adults.
5. Eliminate gender disparities in primary and secondary education by 2015, and achieve gender equality in education by 2015, with a focus on ensuring girls' full and equal access to and achievement in basic education of good quality.

6. Improve all aspects of quality of education and ensuring excellence of all so that recognised and measurable learning outcomes are achieved by all, especially in literacy, numeracy and essential life-skills.[3]

The Dakar Framework for Action on Education for All declared that "no country shall be thwarted from meeting the (Education for All) goals due to a lack of resources".

The second of the eight specific global Millennium Development Goals included in the United Nations Millennium Declaration (2000) reflecting a commitment to "human dignity, equality, and equity", proposed to ensure that by 2015, children everywhere, boys and girls alike, would be able to complete a full course of primary schooling, and, that boys and girls would have equal access to all levels of education.[4] At the UN's Summit on Millennium Goals, 2010, governments recognized the need to provide equitable educational and learning opportunities for all children by addressing the root cause of inequality. And Education For All Global monitoring report,2010, called for the introduction of equity based goals that help focus attention on inequality. At the heart of the education for all agenda is a commitment to increase access to education and to provide high quality education. Under international human rights law, the state is now obliged to be the 'investor of last resort' to ensure that primary education is available to all children. Non-state actors can also undertake to strive for achieving educational goals.

Constitutional Provisions Regarding Education in India

The education system in India is envisaged to meet the constitutional goal of constructing a liberal society based on democracy and social justice. And the constitution that seeks to secure to its citizens justice, liberty, equality and fraternity treated education as an important means of realising the constitutional vision. Hence universalising literacy and elementary education was an inevitable responsibility attached to the fulfilment of the vision.[5] Equal treatment in education for all individuals and communities is an entitlement guaranteed by the constitution.

Articles 29 and 30 of the constitution guarantee the rights of minorities, whether based on religion or language, to establish and administer educational institutions of their choice. The National Policy on Education,1986, stated, "Some minority groups are educationally deprived or backward and suggested to pay greater attention to the education of these groups in the interest of equality and social justice."

Right to Education

The constitution under Article 45 as it stood before the 93rd amendment directed and committed the state to provide free and compulsory education to all children below 14 years of age. 'Not being justiciable this directive failed to prod the Indian state into any kind of concrete action.'[6] In *Unnikrishnan vs. State of Andhra Pradesh,* the Supreme Court pronounced that this article served as a legal source for a 'claim' to education. Subsequently, the 93rd amendment to the constitution, 2001, by inserting Article 21 A to the constitution established the fundamental right to education (though not in absolute sense) with a constitutional guarantee that "the state shall provide free and compulsory education to all children in the age group of 6-14 years. Article 45 was restated to direct the state to provide early childhood care and education for all children until they complete the age of six years. The 93rd Amendment by inserting Article 15(5) to the constitution enables the state to make any special provision, by law, for the advancement of socially and educationally backward classes of citizens, SC, ST, in connection with their admission to educational institutions, including private-aided, unaided, except minority institutions. Now the entitlement to education has become enforceable, and the government can enact laws for caste based reservation in private unaided institutions. Nevertheless, the onus is on the parent or guardian to provide opportunities for education to the child between the age of 6 and 14 years. The realisation of this right requires action, monitoring and commitment from the part of the state as well.

The right to education, however, is different from the other rights enshrined in the constitution since the beneficiary cannot demand this right nor can he/she fight a legal battle for securing this right when it is denied or violated. It is the adult society which must act on behalf of the child. The right to education that India's children have has been commented as precarious.[7]

Article 46 further directs the state to protect the educational and economic interests of the weaker sections of the people, in particular of the scheduled castes and scheduled tribes, and also to protect them from social injustice and all forms of exploitation.

A dynamic, vigorous and bold, inclusive and integrated system of education is sought to ensure by the government through the Right to Education Act (2009). The Right of Children to Free and Compulsory Education Act, 2009, the validity of which was upheld by the Supreme Court, provides for free and compulsory education for all children between the age of 6 and 14. Under the Act, every child in the age group of 6-14 shall have the right to study in a neighbourhood school till completion of elementary education. The Act directs and mandates aided and non-aided schools to provide free and compulsory education to 25 per cent disadvantaged children in their neighbourhoods. Unaided private school managements, except unaided private minority institutions, are required to set apart 25 per cent seats for poor children. Such institutions are obligated to open their doors to students of all social strata, and help students from weaker sections integrate with the others. Henceforth, "school will be rendered a site of social transformation."[8] The Act is a far-going reform measure and has the potential to create a generation of Indians who are equipped to participate in nation-building.[9]

Now the children in India have a right to receive at least eight years of education. What is significant is that by judicial decisions, the right to education has been read into right to life in Article 21. A child who is denied right to access education is not only deprived of his right to live with dignity, he is also deprived of his right to freedom of speech and expression enshrined in Article 19(1) (a).

The 2009 Act seeks to remove all those barriers including financial and psychological barriers which a child belonging to the weaker section and disadvantaged group has to face while seeking admission.[10] "From the scheme of Article 21A and the 2009 Act, it is clear that the primary obligation is of the State to provide free and compulsory education to children between 6 and 14 years and, particularly, to children who are likely to be prevented from pursuing and completing the elementary education due to inability to afford fees or charges." Subject to its economic capacity and development, the state has the obligation to make effective provision for securing the right to education which has been recognised as the gateway from poverty to prosperity, from exclusion to inclusion and from exploitation to emancipation and which protects human rights and enables individuals to lead a life keeping with human dignity.

The Right of Children to Free and Compulsory Education Act, 2009 (RTE Act), however, is not able to achieve the goal of equitable education, without a public funded common school system. Public spending on education is far below what is required to achieve the goal of the right to education for all. Even after the enactment of the Right to Education Act, a common school system recommended by the Education Commission under Professor D. S. Kothari with the objective of promoting equitable education remains a far cry. The scope of the RTE Act providing completely free education is also limited by the provision of the right to levy charges.

National Education Policy

In India, education has been considered as a national priority and given prominence in the development policies. The government is also concerned about making its education system more relevant and develop 'core' or 'key' skills with higher levels and new forms of human capital for the 21st century since education in this century has to operate in a globalised world which is believed to require best educated workforce having competitiveness and efficiency. The areas where the growth sectors require knowledge education has to produce skilled people.

The University Education Report of the *University Education Commission* of 1948-49 (Radhakrishnan Commission) had set the goals for development of higher education: "... to endeavour to relate it to the life, needs and aspirations of the people and thereby make it the powerful instrument of social, economic and cultural transformation necessary for the realization of the national goals. For this purpose, education should be developed so as to increase productivity, achieve social and national integration, accelerate the process of modernization and cultivate social, moral and spiritual values".[11] The Central Advisory Board of Education was set up to define the general aims of educational policy and coordinate the work of various states and universities by guarding against needless duplication and overlapping in the provision of more costly forms of education. The government initiated a planned development of higher education with the establishment of the University Grants Commission in 1953. The Education Commission of 1964-66 (Kothari Commission) examined various aspects of education at all levels and submitted a very comprehensive report full of insight and wisdom. The National Policy on Education, 1968, was mainly based on this report. The NPE-1968 suggested continuous, sustained and intensive effort to expand educational opportunity, to raise the quality of education at all stages, emphasis on the development of science and technology, and the cultivation of moral and social values. It also suggested the education system to produce young men and women of character and ability committed to national service and development, to protect the rights of minorities and promote their educational interests.

Education policies of successive governments stressed the need to provide good quality education at different levels to all segments of society and to ensure inclusiveness through various kinds of interventions. In the mid-1980s, the government initiated a national debate on education by releasing a document titled *The Challenges of Education* which portrayed a picture of stagnation in elementary education, both in terms of the system's reach and quality.

The NPE of 1986 and the Programme of Action 1992 which were based on the reports of the University Education Commission (1948-49) and the Education Commission of 1964-66 (Kothari Commission) continue to provide core elements for government approach towards higher education. The above two reports, in fact, laid down the basic framework for the National Policy for Education in India. The 1986 NPE attempted to formulate an integrated education policy encompassing all levels of education, and sought to provide for a comprehensive policy framework for the development of education. It has delineated the educational goals of Greater Access and Equal Access (equity), Quality and Excellence, Relevance and Promotion of social values to be achieved. It also promised the upgradation of school facilities and the application of child-centred methods among the steps to be taken for enhancing retention and improving quality. The NPE has survived a period of considerable political and cultural anxiety.[12]

At the beginning of the 1990s, the government decided to overcome an acute fiscal crisis by opting for structural adjustment and social safety net policies which brought external financial resources for improving the quality of elementary education and universalising its reach. New approaches and procedures encompassing administrative decentralisation, creation of local-level structures for planning, decision-making and monitoring, and the involvement of non-government organisations were developed. A massive drive to improve school buildings, reorganize the curriculum and recruit and train teachers at the local level was launched.

The Programme of Action 1992 sought to translate these goals into practice. Ninth and tenth plan approach was to place thrust towards addressing the higher education needs of the underrepresented social groups which includes minority candidates. Nonetheless, neither the NPE nor the programme of Action or the successive Plans provided any explicit targets for enrolment expansion.

In his 2011 Independence Day announcements, the then Prime Minister declared the setting up of a Commission "to make suggestions for improvement at all levels of education". And the eleventh plan (2007-2012) was termed virtually a National Education Plan which envisaged growth of inclusive education by providing more educational opportunities to those who are most educationally backward in the country. The plan recognised the importance of higher education, both for social and economic development and meeting the growing needs of the economy and rising aspirations of young people.

The policy objectives were sought to be achieved, by ensuring, among other things, free and compulsory education, equalisation of educational opportunity, by correcting regional and urban-rural imbalances, implementing a common school system, and having special focus on girls and students from backward classes etc...Nevertheless, equality of opportunity in education for all requires the provision of educational services, which will enable the minority community members to maximise their individual talents and make their place within mainstream society.[13]

Inclusive Education

A global initiative on equalisation of opportunity, and education for all, reinforces inclusive education. Inclusive education envisages access to a common schooling for all children, with access to a curriculum appropriate for all. The idea of education as an inclusive process of unleashing the creative potential of diverse groups and individuals, leading to the creation of harmony in society has been emphasised by Yaspal. Eleventh Plan envisaged growth of inclusive education by providing more educational opportunities to the most educationally backward sections. Diversification of education and extension of its reach and coverage must be the focus of education policy to achieve inclusive education.

Communities which were previously excluded from education need to be ensured equal access and opportunities. Such an education is anchored on a system that ensures equality of value and admits all children regardless of the differences in their socio-economic status, and that accepts diversity. The aim of such education is to include all children irrespective of their belonging to particular caste, religion, community, tribe or ethnic group. It is supported by a philosophy built on the belief that all people are equal and should be respected and valued as an issue of basic human rights. Stress is laid on the development of equal opportunity for all.

Inclusive education equates all and is possible in an environment of social and economic equality. Equity in education is important in itself as well as for improving educational status of wider sections of the people. There is complementarity between education expansion and equity. Expansion of education can create opportunities for wider participation of members of various communities in education.

Advancement of education among a large section of the population is an important element of inclusive education as their socio-economic progress and empowerment is linked to this aspect. However, different types of educational institutions engender unequal opportunity which is exclusivist. Moreover, the exorbitant, unbearable, prohibitive fees that some institutions charge as cost to finance education service expenses and other related costs (cost recovery) create barriers to entry of students from poorest households and scuttles inclusive education.

Universal Education

Universal education which envisages common education for all segments of the society is considered essential for the equitable progress of the society. Jose Marti illustrates that education for the masses has saved France; education for the masses holds pleasant Switzerland in respect abroad and in honour at home; education for the masses, solid as well as rancorous in Germany, has given that country its present great power.

In Kerala universal school education has been one of the most important social welfare initiatives. Several programmes were initiated to promote universal education at the national level. The NPE had equated non-formal education with formal schooling as a valid instrument of universalisation of elementary education. District Primary Education Project launched in 1994 aimed at operationalising strategies for achieving universal primary education through District specific planning and disaggregate target setting in female literacy districts. It builds on the successful total literacy campaign which has created favourable climate for universalisation. The Sarva Siksha Abhiyan (SSA) was launched towards the end of the Ninth Plan to achieve a goal of Universal Elementary Education (UEE). The national programme of nutritional support to primary education – mid-day meal programme – was launched in 1995, with the objective of giving a boost to universalisation of primary education by increasing enrolment, retention and attendance and simultaneously improving nutrition of students in primary classes.

Tenth Plan indentified three challenges for achieving universalisation of elementary education:

1. Access to basic education for the unreached segments and social groups;
2. Qualitative improvement in content and processes so as to raise learning achievements;
3. Tackling high drop-outs and low retention rates in primary and upper primary schools.

The present policy, being conceptualised and administered, ignoring the importance of public education, nonetheless, tends to defeat the universalisation agenda.

Government Strategy to Promote Education.

The common minimum programme of the UPA government emphasised the importance of elementary and secondary education. The Approach Paper for the Eleventh Five Year Plan discussed about strategies for improving elementary education. Education at school and higher level was sought to be revamped on a holistic material and systematic basis, with focus on cultivating creativity and intellectual skills aligned to the need of the Indian society and geared to provide vocational/technical/professional education required in the global work place.[14]

There have been several programmes to improve elementary education. The Operation Blackboard scheme started in 1987-88, aimed at improving the classroom environment by providing infrastructure facilities and teaching-learning material. The aim of SSA which was launched as a flagship programme of the Union Ministry of Human Resources Development in 2001-02, was to provide useful and relevant elementary education to all children in the 6-14 age groups by 2010. The programme was supposed to bridge all social, gender and regional gaps with the active participation of the community in the management of schools. One of the main tasks of SSA is to make school more attractive, interesting, and a joyful place. SSA gives importance to early childhood care and education in the 3-6 age group to improve participation of children in the schooling system; this has long been recognised as crucial for the development of emotional, cognitive, sensory and social skills.

To achieve qualitative improvement in secondary education, programmes are initiated focusing on vocationalisation of education, improvement of science education, computer literacy and providing boarding facilities for girls. Under the auspices of National Open School, foundation and secondary and senior secondary level courses, vocational and life enrichment courses are offered.

There has been substantial increase in the allocation of funds to primary education in recent years. Various innovative models to improve access have been tried across Districts. For expansion of school education through DPEP and SSA, the central government provide 75 per cent of funds with the goal of universalising primary education.

Prime Minister's 15 Point Programme for Welfare of Minorities (January, 2006) was an initiative aiming to enhance better access to education and give technical training to improve their skills. The programme sought to give special consideration to the members of the minority communities in filling up posts in "police, railways, nationalised banks and public sector undertakings".

Privatisation of Education: Neo-liberal Influence

The State discharges its obligation to provide education either by establishing and managing educational institutions by the government itself or by aiding, recognising or by granting affiliation to private educational institutions. Since education provides social or public benefits, besides individual benefits, there is public rationale for it. As the contemporary world, characterised by increased international trade, global industries, investment, mobility of people, requires knowledge and skills, there is increasing demand for education to supply qualified trained manpower which can be met by creating more opportunity for education. Privatisation of education has been promoted to meet the need.

That at the government level a consensus regarding a greater role for private sector in higher education exists is evident from the government taking private sector approach to public issues like provision of education service. The Planning Commission favoured to evolve an appropriate policy framework for facilitating greater inflow of private investments in education. The Knowledge Commission (during the United Progressive Alliance Government) favoured to stimulate private investment in education as a means of extending educational opportunities. The above two commissions favoured privatisation of higher education on purely pragmatic grounds. Intellectuals and prominent educationists also seem to favour private investment in higher education, though, restricted to 'a minimum desirable level'.

Since 1990s, government policies encouraged privatisation of education at all levels. The period of economic liberalisation during the 1990s saw a de-emphasis of the role of the state in social and economic life and a greater importance for the private sector and the individual.

World Bank sought to promote a global 'reform agenda' on higher education the key features of which included privatisation, deregulation and marketisation. Market mechanisms are presumed to produce similar results for public services also. Therefore, marketisation is proposed as an effective means to promote more responsive, flexible, efficient results oriented educational institutions. Market fundamentalists champion privatisation and deregulation and treat individuals primarily as consumers. And markets and businesses are presented as the model and solution for all social and individual problems. It is in this framework that the World Bank "reform agenda is oriented to the market rather than to the public ownership or to governmental planning and regulation." Market is used as the sole reference point for judging the worth of an idea or policy on education. Since knowledge and training are so critical as factors in the current political economy, education at every level is being called up on to be market-oriented and market-worthy. And as Basil Bernstein has pointed out "the principles of the market and its managers are more and more the managers of the policy and practices of education. Market relevance is becoming the key orienting criterion for the selection of discourses, their relation to each other, their forms and their research. This movement has profound implications from the primary school to the university. This can be seen in the stress on basic measurable skills at the primary level, vocational courses and specialisations at the secondary level, spurious decentralisation, and the new instruments of state control over higher education and research".[15] The consequence of this pattern is that knowledge is commoditised and student is perceived as a product; and the value system and role of education in advancing equality, dignity of the individual and social justice face unprecedented stress.

Underlying the market orientation of tertiary education is the ascendance, almost worldwide, of market capitalism and the principles of neoliberal economics.[16] Prioritising economic logic is claimed to encourage competition, and to identify the 'best' students or those who do best in the job market. The economic logic was apparent in the conclusion of the Lisbon Special European Council of March, 2000, which underlined the aim to promote, by 2010, 'the most competitive and dynamic knowledge-based economy in the world capable of sustainable economic growth and with more and better jobs and greater social cohesion'.[17] It has been rightly pointed out "surrendering to the logic of economics and of the advantages offered by the big multinationals will not produce the desired results-social justice, equality of opportunity to become self-confident and autonomous to think critically and to be creative."[18]

The World Bank's structural adjustment policies that impose conditionalities for debt relief on third world countries force them to liberalise and downsize higher education. Education is being conducted as if it were a business -'academic capitalism'. In fact, higher education has become a terrain for marketisation agendas. Universities and other institutions are urged to adopt commercial models of knowledge, skills, curriculum, finance, accounting and management organisation in order to warrant state funding and to protect themselves from competitive threats, all as part of the wider neoliberal strategies for reshaping society on the model of a market place. They are now forced to adopt market or market-like strategies to mobilise funds. And education is now being drawn into the world of the market in which educational institutions compete for students and money. Teachers and their traditional protections are identified as the main obstacle to market-based efficiencies. Higher education is rendered less dependent upon teachers' skills; and students are customers or clients.

Facilitating private investments in education has provided a new impetus to commercialising education, although, the 1986 NPE spoke against commercialisation of education, and education is drifting into a market-oriented system in which private providers pursue profit and consumers their own satisfaction. Education is seen as a "commercial product to be bought and sold like any other commodity.[19] This system is usually claimed to provide cheap, widely available, high quality education which will be universally beneficial as Adam Smith has claimed, "self-interest can serve collective interest".

There is a virtual corporatisation in education sector. As a consequence of privatisation, subordination of education to commercial values and vocational skills takes place rapidly. And the value-based relationship between student and educational institutions have changed. Although, there is an element of choice in education, what the evidence suggests is that markets/quasi-markets create inequalities and foster injustice. All these consequences happen counter to the stated objectives of national education policy and are against the objectives of providing equality of opportunity to all in education.

As a follow-up to the extension of liberalisation to education sector there is a move to open higher education sector to foreign agencies. The move is justified as necessary to maintain the standards of higher education within the country as well as to protect the interests of the students and the public. Nonetheless, the fact is that as critics argue, under this privatised condition, 'some schools will cream-off the most able pupils and leave the rest to struggle in 'sink' schools'. Therefore, it is obvious that rather than privatisation, marketisation is the main threat to higher education.

Privatisation of Education

UNESCO distinguishes between public and private education "according to whether a public agency or a private entity has ultimate control over the institution, regardless of the source of funds".[20] Public sector now generally and increasingly delegates responsibility for service delivery to private entities, leaving public organisations with a hollow core. Privatisation opens up public education services to private sector participation on a profit basis. Under the privatisation dispensation the provision of education service is granted to private institutions, enterprises or corporations or trusts. Universities also are encouraged to adopt entrepreneurial practices. They act not only as business partners but also as businesses in themselves and develop profit-making tactics....

Privatisation of education has emerged within government institutions and universities in the form of self-financing courses and private self-financing institutions are also permitted in the education sector.

Rationale for Privatisation

The huge increase in the demand for education, especially, higher education, put high pressure on government to match the demand by corresponding increase in the education infrastructure in terms of educational institutions and other facilities, or to expand the intake capacity of existing educational institutions substantially. The government can evade this responsibility only at risk. Since enrolment on the basis of historical growth pattern is insufficient to meet the growing demand, and the Indian economy needs greater number of skilled and trained graduates, expansion cannot be neglected. Substantial increase in public expenditure on education is required for this purpose. But financial constraints make a heavy toll on education budgets which in turn increases pressure on the state's budget to limit efforts to finance education development. The government presently spends 3.64 per cent of the state income for education. This amounts to 34.88 per cent of state revenue. Expenditure on public education (taken as a percentage of GDP or as a percentage of overall public expenditure) continues to be low in India. By spending less than four per cent of the GDP for education, India is far behind the international norm in spending 6 per cent of the GDP. N.S.S. data shows that the government's share in overall education expenditure has currently undergone steady decline. In Kerala the decline is steep. The need to divide public funds into a variety of sectors and other extra-budgetary commitments are said to constrain government's ability to expand adequately resourced public educational institutions and the same have the consequences of descent in social welfare funding including education. It has been noted that "privatisation can play a useful role in plugging gaps in dwindling public sector budgets and reducing budgetary pressures."[21]

Financial constraints are, in fact, a source of concern in education planning. With the excuse of the state's financial resources on the decline, and the constraint on expenditure, the government turns to the private sector for establishment of educational institutions, and private initiatives are encouraged and supported in massive scale to meet the growing demands of education. Private investors, multinationals, big companies and financial groups are permitted and encouraged to make up for state's shortcomings. And as a result private sector is the fastest growing segment in education, especially in higher education.

The need for private investment in education is now recognised by the government. Advocates of capitalist, liberal form of socio-economic development support, encourage and promote educational institutions under private sector with or without government aid. Persistent expansion of such institutions is motivated primarily by economic considerations favoured by aspiring captains of corporate enterprises. The priority attached to higher education today is for economic reasons, whereas social and political factors were important in the past. In fact, economic rationale has added a new impetus to higher education expansion.[22] The whole educational system is now being re-evaluated in terms of economic competitiveness. Schools are no longer seen as the exclusive preserve of public service or as a state-funded *investment* priority.

Advocates of privatisation also argue that 'government can provide or arrange for citizens to receive a service without actually producing it'.[23] It is the market-oriented principle that treats provision of educational service as characterised by private consumption that defines this approach. By allowing educational programmes under private sector the government proposes to expand educational facilities without extra budgetary allocations. The complex connection between public and private auspices and funding undoubtedly create opportunities in many instances for the expansion of education under private sector in response to the needs of local communities. Higher education viewed primarily as a social experience earlier is now seen as a way to get ahead in life. This culture of aspiration is continuously pushing up the private demand for higher education.[24] The policy-makers are required to respond to this rising demand and they respond by encouraging private sector.

Besides economic reasons, privately-run institutions also thrive on the popular assumption (propaganda) that 'state control of education is bad for quality'. Market theorists, business groups, religious groups, conservative think-tanks and some policy advocates see public education as seriously in trouble, mired in mediocrity and perceive it as rigid and bureaucratic, rule-bound and unaccountable. They propose market-based reforms as solution to these problems. Privatisation is officially claimed to have the effect of improving quality and efficiency as public education is considered of low quality and ineffective. They argue that the competition among private education provider and choice of students to education via privatisation governed by market mechanism, compels the service providers to adequately respond to the needs of the students. The outcome of this responsiveness is a wide variety of educational institutions – a good number of them developed as productive, efficient, high quality, and competitive institutions.

Proponents of market-oriented privatisation see public education, regulated through a top-down system of hierarchical control, wasteful and autocratic. Concentration of power in centralised bureaucracies exercising monopolistic control over fundamental aspects of education – deciding educational needs, planning educational institutions, formulating curriculum, setting standards, controlling service conditions of teachers and their wages, help the bureaucrats to further enhance their power and prestige rather than educational progress of the public. Access to the education bureaucracy is difficult for majority of students and their parents.

A heavy reliance on private institutions is seen as an indication of public systems not performing adequately. In the words of Professor Poonam Batra, "Too often dysfunctionality characterises public systems of formal education." In response, private players step in to meet the demand for quality education. It is obvious that privatisation can be a direct consequence of a dysfunctional public education system. Private schools are claimed as richly rewarding as they could deliver academically robust learning to their students, develop their character and promise high returns to their future success. They claim or are believed to provide more attractive and inspiring environment to learn, minimise class-room distraction, re-assure discipline and structure, ensure teachers' high involvement and opportunities to motivate students to improve their academic performance, ensure accountability from teachers towards the success of each individual student. Those students emerge with high level of qualification and a sense of purpose, more rounded, more holistically prepared and ready to withstand and face the world. It is also argued that private sector institutions may provide the necessary dynamism, and respond to the increasing demand for professional courses, to meet the requirement of skills and competences required by the present world.[25] This trend, however, results in indiscriminate mushrooming of unplanned and unregulated private institutions as well as teacher training institutions.

Cost Recovery

Public education's major concern is resource deficit/resource inequality which is not addressed to ensure equitable education to all. The excess demand for education and contracting resources let the government to justify/legitimise charging user fees to raise additional revenues so as to expand service provisions. When public needs of education were not met by public institutions, private providers cherishing market orientation stepped in to provide education, but unilaterally and surreptitiously decided and imposed high cost of education which the student has to bear. The cost of education is not collectively determined by the private education provider and the students. This paved the way for collection of hefty amounts as capitation fees etc. by private education service providers. Advancing of community interest is not the primary objective of the private sector, nor a motivational factor, but only a by-product. It is by impairing public education system's objective of serving the collective public and facilitating of equitable distribution of educational opportunities to all education seekers that the private sector gains. It is to be noted that the Birla-Ambani Report-2000, while suggesting private universities favoured enforcement of user-pay principle in higher education. Further, the collection of higher fees is sought to be justified on the argument that "offering a service for a price gives important information about what consumers will pay for, even if the charges are only a fraction of the cost of providing the service".[26] Education is treated as a private good, that is, a service that can be consumed in individual units like the market regulated exchange of goods and services. It is usual that like any enterprise, private educational institutions with better facilities and faculties' higher premiums facilitate only the superior class to take advantage of such institutions. That privatisation and market mechanisms in education favour privileged classes with high socio-economic status and sustains their domination and hierarchies is obvious here. This makes the market-oriented private sector education system divisive along privileged and less privileged. An education service for which the students bear the burden of cost is unlikely to inculcate ideal social relations to construct shared values that enrich and transform communities.

This change brought in the education structure tends to end in marketisation of education, reduces the share of state funding in education, and leads to erosion of state responsibility to create sustainable systemic provisions for basic education[27]. This change against public interest also institutionalises prevalent inequities in terms of access to quality education, subordinates education to commercial values and vocational skills.

The ill-consequences of privatisation of education are described by Prabhat Patnaik: Substantial privatisation of higher education would create 'organic intellectuals for the global job market', rather than creating 'organic intellectuals of the people for individual thinking'.[28]

There is no credible effort/policy initiative to bring systemic reforms to promote/ensure a decent common education system."

Kerala Education Profile

In Kerala, education in the pre independent period was not inclusive, but was a privilege for the rich, elite and upper class people. The educational system was decidedly elitist and class dominated in character. Equality in education opportunity was non-existent. Disparities between inter-caste, inter-religious, rural-urban, male-female and occupation groups were rampant. The poor and backward were educationally low achievers. The SCs, STs and Muslims suffered most from lack of equal access to education. Yet the erstwhile Travancore had initiated an education policy which envisaged the state defray the cost of education.

After independence the need for popular education extending educational opportunities to all sections of society was given importance as stressed in the constitution of India. Popular education envisaging education for all was developed as the governments pursued a general policy of education. The hierarchical-inequitous principle of distribution of educational opportunities that hitherto existed was sought to be eliminated. Thus, in a sense, democratisation in education gained momentum.

Today, Kerala has a record of creditable achievement in education and literacy. Schools have been part of Kerala's social life and contribute positively and significantly to the development of its society. This certainly helped the state to surge ahead of many other States in Human Development Indicators.

The state ranked very high in overall enrolment, but exhibited markedly different pattern in producing the aggregate outcome. It leads in enrolments at the primary, secondary school level, and is third in higher education enrolment but drops to seventh in the per cent of school pupils enrolled in technical or vocational programmes.[29] And education for the backward classes and minority communities, especially the members of the minority Muslim community, who were excluded from education, was one agenda in the social-political struggles for equality in social, economic and political spheres of Kerala's life.

Public Education in Kerala

Public provisioning of education facilities has long been a fundamental feature of the development paradigm in Kerala. Almost all the social reforms and political movements in the state have encouraged school education as an effective tool against caste, gender and class discrimination. The emphasis on, and great demand for human capital, made a case for greater public investment in education. Nonetheless, government's education policy emphasised on a combination of public and private initiatives at all levels of education. And government and private-aided schools and colleges had been the backbone of the state's public education system. Education was sought to be promoted as a universal privilege for children protecting them from distressful human conditions of inequalities and injustices. Universal education funded by the state, was an objective of state policy. The education costs of students in private educational institutions, categorised as aided educational institutions, are borne by the government. These private institutions, however, exercise control over appointment of teachers, and have quota of seats with regard to admission of students. A great majority of such institutions, including professional institutions, are affiliated to forward and advanced religious and caste groups. Religious/caste and community-based organisations viz. NSS, SNDP, MES, the churches of various denominations like the Syrian Christian Church and other Christian organisations vie with each other to seize the opportunities for establishing educational institutions under private sector. Almost 80 per cent of educational institutions are now being controlled by these community organisations.

A great majority of private educational institutions that do not receive any financial support from the government (known as self-financing institutions) are also controlled by such groups and individuals. As a result educational institutions in the state have become a powerful vested interest, and 'represent' powerful communities. Organised educational interests by themselves or under the direction of these organised communities have been able to capture over one-third of Kerala's revenue budget.[30] Public spending on education in Kerala was the highest in India. University and college education are not free, but heavily subsidised.

Despite the importance given earlier to public education, the current public education services are inadequate and the quality is poor in terms of students' academic achievement especially in rural areas. Public schools in urban centres also are not better. Not all students leave schools and colleges well equipped with necessary skills, they need to develop a secure livelihood and to participate in social, economic and political life efficaciously.

Education programmes in Kerala, nonetheless, suffer from insufficient funding, iniquitous orientation and lack of integrated planning. Although the 2011-12 budget proposed to raise the outlay on education by 24 per cent of government budgetary support, per student expenditure was slashed by government. Expansion of bureaucracy and extra-budgetary commitments act as constraints on allocation for education. In fact, education funding as a portion of total government spending tends to decrease. This results in increased individual burden for continuing education. Therefore, the need for state increasing allocation for education as a political priority is very high. Public funding for education is indispensable for development of human potential, and increased expenditure on education is required to benefit from the global economy.

In general inadequate infrastructure in public schools, irrational teacher-student ratio, and low level of teacher dedication, commitment and performance are some of the problems in primary as well as secondary education in the state. Partisan teacher politics has its dent in schools. Partisan attitude in schools and colleges scuttles promotion of mutual respect, tolerance and critical thinking, and reinforces disrespect, intolerance and prejudice pushing sometimes the Kerala society into social conflicts.

Privatisation Galore in Kerala

The education system in Kerala embracing an intermingling of public and private aspects and funding inducts private agencies too, along with public institutions, to provide education to the public. The last two decades witnessed unprecedented increase in privatisation of education, with new ways of funding. Perhaps, there are intense and rampant attempts to privatise education. This trend permeates to all sectors of education, impinging on the professed policy of equitous education.

And the state has a huge and rapidly expanding new variety of private sector education system – self-financing – both under private as well as public sectors. In fact, 86.4 per cent of seats in the engineering colleges are in the private sector and 84 per cent of the engineering colleges are in the self-financing sector.

Prodigious demand for education at all levels as well as concerns over education quality pushed many children to seek private sector education. Until 2000, the seats available in the few government-run engineering and medical colleges in Kerala were far too inadequate for the ever-increasing demand for professional college seats in the state and there was a steady flow of students and resources to the mushrooming self-financing colleges in neighbouring states. Perhaps, a strong ideological lobby which favours privatisation too has grown with tacit political support and endorsement. And, the government saw privatisation as a real option. The avowed policy of government, in fact, was to encourage more private investment in education, especially in professional education sector. In this background, the government opened the doors for large-scale private investment in the sector, claiming it as a measure to help the large number of students to find the educational opportunities of their choice in the state itself. The government itself has started 'self-financing' educational institutions in the cooperative sector and under government controlled autonomous bodies like Institute of Human Resource Development and Lal Bahadur Shastri Centre, besides Centres of Universities. In fact, the education sector is dominated by recognised and affiliated self-financing private institutions in which the service receiver (consumer) is required to pay for the education service which imposes heavy financial burden on the parents, particularly of poor households. Such institutions remain inaccessible for poor backward citizens, especially of minority communities. This system creating deep disparities in opportunities for education which is linked to wealth is apparent.

Policy declarations in this respect, however, averred that the principles of equity and social justice that had been the cornerstone of the State's education sector until then would continue to guide it in the new era of large-scale private investment too.[31] The main policy statement emphasised that the sanctioning of two self-financing professional colleges would be equivalent to the government establishing a college of its own, because 50 per cent of seats in such institutions were envisaged to be filled from the government merit-list prepared on the basis of a common entrance examination conducted by the Entrance Commissioner and for students gaining admission in these seats, the same fee in the government colleges was proposed. Based on this understanding, though not as part of any written contract that the essentiality certificates were issued to the managements of the self-financing colleges.

The private sector in school as well as in higher education including professional education has grown quite substantially and rapidly over the last two decades and has become commercial. The state has been experiencing a mushrooming increase in the number of private educational institutions which are run by collecting prohibitively exorbitant rates of fees including capitation fee, beyond the prescribed norm, in surreptitious and unjust ways from students. Although, the Prohibition of Unfair Practices in Technical and Medical Institutions and Universities Act, 2010, seeks to rein in private professional education, it fails to address the larger issue of social justice and excellence in education.

Court Facilitates Freedom of the Private Sector

The Supreme Court judgement in the T.M.A. Pai Foundation case that redefined the rights of the minorities to establish and run educational institutions of their choice but declared unconstitutional the provision in the Unnikrishnan case (1993) that obliged the students who secured admission under payment quota to subsidise the cost of education of those admitted in the merit quota was in favour of the private sector.

The government order, fixing norms for admission and payment of fees in unaided professional colleges, was declared arbitrary and illegal by the Kerala High Court. This was in line with the Supreme Court ruling in 2003, in the Islamic Academy of Education case, against the government fixing a rigid fee structure in self-financing colleges and directing the government to allow the management's sufficient discretion in admitting students.

Now the fee for a student for medical course is invariably from 25 to 50 lakhs. Although the court ruled in favour of merit as the criterion for admission and warned against profiteering and charging of capitation fees by the self-financing institutions, the principle of equity and justice suffered a beating. The Yaspal Committee, expressing concern on the mushrooming of engineering and management colleges, that had "largely become business entities dispensing very poor quality education" expressed doubt about the source of funding of private education providers, and said that it was either unaccounted wealth from business and political enterprises or from capitation fee. It is apparent that private investment/Foreign Direct Investment in education promotes commercialisation of education.

Government efforts to rein the self-financing managements have not been successful till today. And the state continues to have the iniquitous system of education which denies access to the disadvantaged and less privileged sections of the society.

The fleecing of students by self-financing professional colleges exploiting loopholes in the law related to those institutions and the inability of the government to check it has been a matter of concern in Kerala. The discriminatory admission practices and exorbitantly high fees charged from the students, denying admission to meritorious and poor students, would have socially harmful effects. Such institutions are least concerned about fulfilling the minimum quality requirement stipulated by the UGC/AICTE or Medical Council, and are not committed to attracting and retaining permanent teachers with high qualifications and research experience and to provide them with the necessary skills and support. And cronyism rules appointments. Many of the self-financing institutions are unable to provide even minimum competent faculty strength and are of low performance and inferior standard. They, in fact, suffer from deficient physical and academic infrastructure and academic quality.

Asymmetrical System

Private recognised and self-financing educational institutions are predominantly urban-centred. Kendriya Vidyalayas have only nominal presence in the state. There is a vast difference between central schools and those run by state government and local government institutions in the matter of infrastructural facilities, funds utilisation etc. The implementation of a common schooling is very difficult and will encounter problems in Kerala's stratified and socially and economically divided society.

Rural areas have little access to efficiently run institutions. Notwithstanding some exceptions, public schools in Kerala in general are perceived as not effectively educating the poor, especially the rural poor. The survey result shows public preference for private schools. This problem is compounded by the situation of insufficient, poor infrastructure, teacher delinquency, ineffectiveness, neglect, evasion of commitment etc. Disparity in access to quality education and educational accomplishments between the rich and the poor, and rural and urban sections also persists. As Andre Beteille observed, "Even after elementary education has become universal, inequalities will remain in the quality of what is available to children from the different strata of society. Even at the level of elementary education universality does not mean equality".[32] And despite attaining universalisation of literacy, equality of access to education is elusive in Kerala. Since women education also suffer because of the inability of parents to pay higher fees for their education, gender disparity is not decreasing substantially, although gender education is advancing.

Privatisation of education, in fact, distorts the concept of universal and inclusive education and defeats the goal of education for all. It creates different types of education among various sections of society which is catastrophic to the principle of equity. There are other distressful areas in the education structure of Kerala. Vocational education which is made part of secondary education intended to prepare students for employment by creating skilled man-power, is not functioning efficiently. It hardly helps in improving the employment potential of students who undergo or are trained in vocational courses.

The existing system of education is not free from alien values and methods; it carries with it alien culture and ways of life which tends to create selfdom. The curriculum barely helps in bringing about social transformation accompanying virtues of truth, patience, tolerance, mutuality, cooperativeness etc. The respect for labour has also been vanishing from the present system of education.

Public school curriculum that requires all children to follow is not suited to all of them to meet their needs. The curriculum is barely planned to hold the child's interest and the child develops distaste for various subjects is very much apparent. The teaching practices hardly facilitate the expression of originality. The child is being suffocated and intellect robbed.

To borrow the comment of Jose Marti, "This sterile repugnant uniformity is a kind of intellectual livery. It produces cold, stupid children, drop out of school with uncultivated tastes and no thirst for knowledge, lacking the grace of childhood and the enthusiasm of youth."[33] This is why education sector in Kerala seems struggling to meet the challenges of the knowledge revolution.

Future education policies must pay attention to the above discussed concerns and also poverty-related issues like hunger, malnutrition and sustained earning which are pre-requisites for quality education, and address local/regional imbalances in educational facilities and quality, resource constraints, inadequate physical infrastructure, intriguing academic climate, bureaucratisation etc. which are problems that affect education. Also issues like early childhood care—an important component of the Dakar framework—poverty-induced conditions like child labour and drop-out must also be addressed, because they are as important as school facilities, curriculum and pedagogy for quality improvement.

Notes and References

1. *See* Human Development Report, 2010, The Real Wealth of Nation: Pathways to Human Development, Twentieth Anniversary Edition, United Nation's Development Programme, 2010.
2. *See* Education for All: Meeting Our Collective Commitments, text adopted by the World Education Forum, Dakar, Senegal, April 26-28, 2000.
3. http://www.unesco.org/en/efa/efa-goals, July 19, 2010.
4. http://www.un.org/millenniumgoals
5. Krishna Kumar, '*Quality of Education at the Beginning of 21st Century*', *Lessons from India,* Central Institute of Education, New Delhi, p. 14.
6. Making RTE work, *The Hindu,* April 3, 2010.
7. *See* Krishna Kumar, India's children have a precarious right, *The Hindu,* April 3, 2010, p. 8.

8. Manabi Majumdar and Jos Mooij, In pursuit of socially mixed schools, *The Hindu*, May 5, 2012, p. 10.
9. *The Hindu*, Editorial, April 13, 2012, p. 10.
10. Quoted from *The Hindu*, April 13, 2012.
11. *See* Sukhadeo Thorat, 'Higher Education in India: Emerging Issues Related to Access, Inclusiveness and Quality', Nehru Memorial Lecture, University of Mumbai, Mumbai, November 24, 2006.
12. Krishna Kumar, *Ibid.*, p.15.
13. K.G. Kannabiran, An Unfortunate Decision in AP, *The New Indian Express*, February 10, 2010.
14. Kapil Sibal, the then Human Resource Minister, delivering the Convocation Address at Pondicherry University, *The Hindu*, April 3, 2010, p. 7.
15. Basil Benstein, *Pedagogy, Symbolic Control and Identity*, Taylor and Francis, London, 1996, p.87; Quoted by Krishna Kumar, Quality of Education at the Beginning of 21st Century, Lessons from India, Central Institute of Education, New Delhi.
16. Johnstone, D.B., Arora, A., and Expert on, W, *The Financing and Management of Higher Education*: A Status Report on World Wide Reforms. Washington DC: World Bank Departmental Working Paper, http://www-wdsworldbank.org
17. Quoted in Tariq Ramadan (2010), *The Quest for Meaning: Developing a Philosophy of Pluralism*, Penguin Books, London, p. 134.
18. Tariq Ramadan, *Ibid.*, p. 136.
19. Newman, F., Couturier, L. and Scurry J. (2004), *"The Globalization of Higher Education"*, at http// ctl.stanford.edu
20. UNESCO; 2007a:46.
21. Oxfam International, 2002, Education Now! Report, Oxfam, London.
22. Pawan Aggarwal (2009), *Indian Higher Education*, Sage, New Delhi, p. 42.
23. Savos, E.S. (1987), *Privatisation: The Key to Better Government*, Chatham, N.J: Chatham House, pp. 60-61.
24. Pawan Aggarwal, p. 172.
25. *See* Pawan Agarwal, *Ibid.*, pp. 436-437.
26. *See* Richard Rose, (1989) Charges as Contested Signals, *Journal of Public Policy*, July 9, September 1989, pp. 261-86 quoted by Kenneth Godwin, Using Market based Incentives to Empower the Poor, in Helen Ingram Steven and Rathgeb Smith (Eds.) (1995), Public Policy for Democracy, Frank Bros. and Co., Noida, p. 167.
27. Janet R. Dickson *et al.*, (2010), *Advancing Global Education: Patterns of Potential Human Progress*, Vol. II, Oxford University Press, p. 48.
28. At the Foundation Day Lecture of "NUEPA" Alternative Perspectives on Higher Education in the context of Globalization in 2007, Quoted in Pawan Agarwal, p. 49.

29. Lloyd I. Rudolph and Susanne Hoeber Rudolph, Regional Patterns of Education: Rimland and Heartland in Indian Education In Rudolph and Susanne Hoeber Rudolph, *Explaining Indian Democracy: A Fifty Year Perspective,* 1956-2006—The Realm of the Public Sphere: Identity and Policy, Oxford University Press, 2008, p. 68.
30. Lloyd I. Rudolph and Susanne Hoeber Rudolph, *op cit.,* p. 67.
31. R. Krishnakumar, The Price of Education, *Frontline,* July 29, 2005, pp. 31-32.
32. Andre Beteille (2001), Equality and Universality, *Economic and Political Weekly,* (36:38), p. 3625.
33. *See* Jose Marti, *op cit.,* pp. 15-16.

5

Socio-Economic Profile and Educational Status

Muslim Community in Kerala

Educational, social, political, cultural and economic factors are integral ingredients in the development of a community. Prevalence of education and availability of intellectual and technical skills, which varies among different people/communities at different socio-economic levels, are crucial in this respect. Educational progress of a community is determined by its increasing participation rates or flows of individuals into, through and out of components of education systems.[1] Among all socio-religious communities or under-served groups, Muslims have been found most educationally backward with low educational attainment; the most deprived, marginalised, neglected, discriminated, excluded and powerless community at the national level. The worst thing the Muslim community suffers from is shortage of intellectuals and educationally and technically competent persons. And extreme powerlessness is a constant feature of backward Muslim households. Social backwardness, in terms of the inability to access equal opportunity in education and employment is a key concern of the community.

In 1983, Dr. Gopal Singh, Chairman of the High Power Committee set up to enquire into the conditions of SCs, STs and religious minorities found Muslims and Neo-Buddhists as most educationally backward communities at the national level. It was in 1986, for the first time since independence, the government of India declared that Indian Muslims were educationally backward and government of India declared the community "National Educationally Backward Minority" in 1993, and the report of Prime Minister's High Level Committee on Muslims under the chairmanship of Justice (retired) Rajinder Sachar (appointed to enquire into the status of Muslims in India) depicts the true picture of the social, economic and educational status of the Muslim community in India. The committee highlighted very sharply the relative deprivation of "India's largest minority group, the Muslims, in the field of education as well as in different spheres, and in terms of levels of living and human development conditions. The report established the fact that the Muslims in India have been left out of the development trajectory" and found the community the most deprived and at a twofold disadvantage with low levels of education combined with low quality education. Thorat and Newman affirmed that Muslims like other social classes – tribes, Dalits etc. had only low expectations as they suffered from similar disadvantages suffered by the tribes and Dalits. The Indian government suggest that Muslims suffer political and institutional disadvantage[2] as the Dalits and Adivasi communities.

A comparison of educational status of Hindu-Muslim communities points towards a trend of Muslims lagging in literacy levels and educational attainments, regarded as a pre-requisite for social and economic development. Muslim school completion rate is lower than that of Hindu and Christian community members. The case of higher education is not different. Backward and marginalised among the Muslims continue to suffer from lower access to higher education as compared with other advanced counterparts from their own religion. In the socio-economic sphere, Muslims occupy 'a niche position characterised by self-employment in petty business, and fall behind Hindus and Christians in access to education and formal sector jobs.'[3] On the other hand, members of some forward caste/community groups who dominate education sector also dominate public life and government institutions/positions. Lack of education or deficit in proper higher/professional education holds back the Muslims in the matter of regular salaried employment in higher coveted positions.

It has been found that a number of factors including historical and social prejudices, socio-economic development lag, and de facto segregation/exclusion operated to impede the members of the community from attainment of equality of opportunity for their children in the educational context. Education of large section of the community was disrupted by several socio-economic factors – poverty, increase in education expenses, lack of motivation, low expectation, lack of confidence about the reward from education etc. They were victims of multiple disparities across the state, between rural-urban, inter-caste, inter-religious groups. They suffered under a hierarchical and uneven pattern of distribution of educational opportunities in which education was a privilege which usually went with the forward communities and the elites. Limited access to good quality schools in the neighbourhood is a major problem that affects education of female Muslim students more adversely.

Among the religious groups, General Enrolment Ratio is lowest among the Muslims (8.19 per cent) compared with Christian, Jain, Sikh and forward Hindu groups. GER of OBC Muslims was 7 per cent as compared with 9 per cent for other Muslims. Similar differences are observed in the case of Eligible Enrolment Ratio (EER). For OBC Muslims EER is 50.16 per cent as compared with 63 per cent of other Muslims. Muslim community in general is one of the groups, particularly the female from this community, who suffered most from lack of access to education, particularly higher education.

The educational inequalities – a function of low levels of overall educational attainment[4] and economic disparities, social inequalities and discrimination restricted them complete citizenship rights. Low socio-economic status perpetuates poor education which affects the social and economic life of the Muslim community. They are socially, economically and culturally disadvantaged.

Discrimination and communalisation of the atmosphere that prevailed in schools run by other communities added to the problem[5] of inequality in education attainment. As Dreze and Sen observe that stratification in Indian society is reflected in inequalities in educational attainment across caste, religion and ethnic boundaries.[6] "Recent discussions emphasise that Muslims may have self-selected out of the public education system because of its 'sanskritisation' so that issues of religious and political identities are conflated with educational demand."[7] Perception of discrimination has led to a sense of alienation among the members of the community. This is seen by the community as a cause of inequality. Jeffrey and Jeffrey argued that many Muslims regarded their relative (economic) weaknesses as stemming from anti-Muslim discriminatory practices. Studies by Thorat and Newman confirmed the contemporary patterns of economic discrimination, and particularly discrimination in non-market transactions like access to education faced by Dalits and religious minorities like Muslims, and the underlying attitudinal orientations that contribute to inequality in various spheres of life.[8] The low representation of Muslims in public or private sector employment and the perception of discrimination in securing salaried jobs make them give less importance to formal 'secular' education...[9] In the perception of Sachar committee, Muslims do not see education as necessarily translating into formal employment. Perception of low returns as well as discrimination deters Muslim men from pursuing higher education. The belief that their sons would not get jobs led Muslim parents to devalue the importance of education as an instrument of upward socio-economic mobility.[10] That the recruitment system also was discriminatory is obvious. As a consequence majority of Muslim men are found in low income, low dignity, hard and tiresome jobs. It is largely the members of urban based, highly educated upper middle class sections who manage to make it to top jobs in the modern high profile government and corporate sector. This situation adversely affects the integration of backward, disadvantaged Muslims into the social, political, economic and cultural processes and the mainstream of development which is crucial to empower them.

The situation in Kerala is more or less comparable to that is available at the national level, although, perceptible but moderate progress is visible in some spheres of socio-economic life of the Muslim community. The following part probes the socio-economic, particularly educational status of the members of the Muslim community in Kerala. In this process, this chapter focuses on the question of how the community is deficit/backward in social, political, educational and economic status and devoid of elements of self-worth, self-esteem and capacity to handle their life's problems, and to change their social constructions which disable them. Given the present not- so-impressive socio-economic and educational status of the community and the great and persistent challenges that need to be overcome, it is suggested that the members of the community need to take great strides towards the goal of removing their social backwardness which alone will facilitate empowerment.

The methodology adopted here is descriptive, besides drawing from household survey results.

Status of Muslims in Kerala: Factors Responsible for their Educational Backwardness

Muslims in Kerala, constituting 24.2 per cent of the state's population and the largest minority community, are enumerated within the category of Socially and Educationally Backward Classes, based on the factual assessment of their socio-economic status. In fact, the Muslim community in Kerala suffered a constant shortfall in educational attainment and lagged greatly behind forward Hindu and Christian communities socially, educationally and economically. Marked variations in educational attainment/ status of different social classes/groups and their participation in education within the state is still a distressful factor. The spread of education in other socio-religious communities also tends to outpace the educational progress among the Muslims. The educational gap between different social classes—Muslims and forward Hindu and Christian groups—in the matter of achievement of education has been too wide and is not reducing. The educational status of Muslims in certain areas, particularly in coastal and other backward rural areas is very seriously low. Indicators such as access to quality and delivery in terms of education service that determine the education attainment of communities are very low in their case. Notwithstanding the rise in the overall education level of the Muslim community and the significant progress in the education sector in contemporary Kerala, Muslim disadvantage in education continues with lower level educational endowments and earnings. The effect of recent improvement in enrolment rate of Muslim children for primary education is being neutralised by the increasing drop-outs before completing secondary education. The education 'stocks'[11] (education attainment levels) of the Muslim community is also short of the desired levels, and lower than that is achieved by members of forward Hindu and Christian communities. This has been a major factor that affected their social status.

Left out of the state's progress record for long and cut off from the mainstream of socio-economic life they have not been able to fully catch up with members of forward communities who have higher educational attainment, employment record, government service, representation in defence and police forces.

Having achieved not so promising social development, the community is mired in a trajectory of education deficit and as a result largely excluded from full, efficacious participation in the social, political and economic life of the state. In fact, the prospects for progress of the community were hindered by household educational disadvantages.

The reasons for the disadvantages and backwardness of the Muslims, as elsewhere, are historical, social and economic. They face multifaceted issues, ranging from problems related to poverty, marginalisation, exclusion, discrimination, social disabilities, large size of the family, lack of opportunities, and inequity which are barriers in their educational participation and educational progress. Lack of support to pursue education and various forms of socio-economic exclusion in the past were also barriers. Their low profile was, in fact, caused /precipitated by the difficulty or inability of an overwhelming majority of the community members to secure easy and equal access to education and employment.

Because of skewed distribution of education service most of the marginalised and disadvantaged sections who are in greatest need of education are unable to access it. Lack of good quality educational institutions in the neighbourhood which hindered enrolment was a problem that could not have overcome easily. The religious schools (Madrassas) barely provide general education, understanding of science, nor focus on necessary skill development. The primary education that some Muslim students get at the Madrassas is invariably of poor standard which renders mainstreaming for secondary education difficult.

The British rule had deleterious effect in the educational progress of Muslims, especially in the Malabar region in Kerala, where there is significant presence of Muslim population. Muslim enrolment was abysmally the lowest during this period. The impact of British rule, particularly its differential effects on different regions...... accentuated established differences and introduced new ones that were inter alia highly salient for education.[12] The introduction of English education was among the most important of the forces that sharpened class differences.

Moreover, active involvement in the freedom struggle, particularly *Mappila Rebellion* and the consequent oppression by the British rulers disrupted the steady path of development of education among the Muslim population of Malabar region. This made the Muslim community remain deprived in the social, economic and political sphere for long. The way a section of the uninformed members of the community perceived/perceives education had/has an overall impact on their progress/digress in education. Traditional barriers and conservative, orthodox and obscurantist views and attitude of Muslim men towards women education prevented and still prevent women from going out of their homes to pursue education, especially after high school, and acquire modern education. Neglect of women's education and their low status in the community was a factor that tended to pull the community further backward.

Distaste of members of the community towards modern education because of low expectations of rewards, limited access to better jobs or lack of confidence in acquiring employment, orthodoxy in belief systems etc. also contributed to their ignoring education and low level of education attainment, although the community now looks at education as a means of improving its socio-economic status.

Communally and politically sensitive and hostile environment and the social discrimination processes that prevailed in some parts of Kerala made the members of the Muslim community vulnerable and tended to disrupt or digress education of their children. Lack of equality and social justice in almost all walks of life, including education, of the traditional Kerala society that also defined government policies affected the educational progress of the backward communities in general, and that of the Muslim community in particular. Control of majority of educational institutions by forward socio-religious groups tended to deny the Muslim students substantive equality of opportunity in educational participation. And these institutions (owned and managed by caste/religious groups) seldom had practices or social relations that helped engender community sense. In some of such institutions, the environment and some of the practices even engendered anti-community relations. The problems linked to inequality and imbalances in educational attainment that the community faced, in fact, tended to perpetuate community divide and exclusionary habits, and domination of the less privileged by the privileged and powerful ones. The domination manifested in political, administrative, economic, and social spheres and impinged on mutuality and complementarities in diverse social actions. The backward poor Muslim members were victims of these developments.

Inequality that existed within the state mirrors the societal divide in education. They were victims of the inequalities that existed in status, resources, employment and power. Discrimination was pervasive in educational services and employment. They suffered discrimination with regard to access/admission to educational institutions majority of which were controlled and managed predominantly by other social groups. Muslim children widely remained at disadvantageous position when they attended schools which were dominated by children of the forward sections. The near absence of Muslim teachers in an overwhelming majority of schools and colleges had the outcome of Muslim students remaining distanced from their teachers which affected their empowerment.

Where equality of opportunity required the provision of educational and employment services to enable the members of a backward community to maximise their individual talents and take their place within mainstream society, the Muslims remained deprived of such services to a great extent. They were a target of inequality of conditions, privileges and elitism thrust up on society in the past.

Economic and social backwardness significantly affected the community's ability to advance education participation and attainment. Since educational attainment is strongly associated with wealth, and other factors that can lead to disadvantage,[13] economic deprivation and disparity, and class differentiations had negative impact on the community's educational advancement and empowerment. Due to lack of sufficient financial resources to meet the educational expenses, and preoccupation with livelihood activities the educational trajectory of the poor Muslim students was interrupted which ultimately created inequalities in educational pathways and experiences. Preoccupied with their routine works for livelihood earnings, large sections of Muslim community members with a background of poor socio-economic level had little enthusiasm/interest in having any formal education for their children, but had only less positive attitudes or motivation towards education. With higher level of unemployment and low earnings, education of community members was neglected or abandoned.

Financial constraints have driven the students out of schools and colleges to earn by doing low paid, low status works. Parents used to take children out of schools and sent them to work in the informal economy, markets, shops, hotels, groceries etc. which carried low status. Being a casual-petty wage worker/day labourer or doing petty street/market vending of articles is largely the preserve of poorly educated Muslim men in Kerala. Those who are in regular and highly paid employment are very trivial, and constituted from highly educated middle and upper middle and high classes. Muslim concentration in self-employment keeps the Muslim students with lower educational attainment. A large part of Muslim hindrance in the jobs market stemmed from the difficulty that Muslims had in finding regular employment. Compared to forward Hindu and Christian community members who had better access to regular jobs, Muslims suffered from considerable access disadvantage in terms of obtaining regular employment,[14] especially in private/corporate sector. In this respect, the community, in general, remained excluded or handicapped because of lower educational achievement, although a large proportion of them are working poorly.

Low education level of parents was a detracting factor in children's participation.

Uncertainty in the matter of opportunity for employment according to the qualification acquired provided less motivation or incentive for higher education among poor children. The community had not been successful in motivating and helping such children to pursue higher education as the community had not much resources under its disposal and the majority of educational institutions having the trappings of minority label were controlled and managed by individuals or trusts controlled by family members, who had vested interests. The observations contained in the Rajinder Sachar Committee Report that "Muslims do not see education as necessarily translating into formal employment" and that "the low representation of Muslims in public or private sector employment and the perception of discrimination in securing salaried jobs" make them give less importance to formal 'secular education' is true to a great extent in the case of less educated, tradition bound orthodox Muslims in some parts of Kerala, especially in northern districts.

All the above discussed facts hampered the education of the members of the community, affected their ability to acquire higher education and held the community back in its aspiration for education completion, particularly long-term educational prospects.

Asymmetry in Education Attainment

Uneven distribution of educational opportunities and advantages and higher cost of education render access to education to large section of the community difficult. This results in dramatic variance in educational (especially higher and professional level) attainment of different sections of people and their educational goals remain unrealised due to lack of ability to accomplish them. While children of lower standard of living and lower income have significantly lower educational attainment, it is the children of the middle class, upper middle class and higher classes who benefit largely and indiscriminately from educational programmes. Only children of well-off sections access resource rich and competent institutions, children from socially marginalised and economically deprived are left out to depend on resource-poor and poor quality dysfunctional public schools. Although, expansion of schools and other higher educational institutions have facilitated physical access, the low quality of many of them limits access to learning and thus lowers the access and completion rates of education for poor Muslim children. For the disadvantaged, education thus become yet another form of oppression and social exclusion.[15] However, urbanites do fare somewhat better and sections among the members of the community who have been able to gain economic prosperity also have been able to increase educational advancement of their children.

The common entrance test for admission to professional courses weighs so heavily against the students from poor socio-economic and rural background. Access to engineering, medical and management courses is almost difficult for the poor. This is also responsible for their inability to secure good jobs today. The recent studies have established the fact that "those who manage to get top jobs in the IT industry and other high profile private sector companies are mostly of urban, upper middle class background that get good education." It is their class position that enables them to acquire such education.

Poor Muslim students being relatively less advantaged in the matter of access to higher/professional education are disadvantaged in access to other social goods that includes political, cultural, and economic. They have only low and insignificant representation in government, public sector undertakings, banks, railways, paramilitary forces, police, defence etc. In the period that preceded and that followed independence, Muslims in Kerala had no access to good jobs in the formal sector which was a barrier to their acquiring good educational qualifications. In formal and informal public sector and private enterprises, the Muslims are in inferior jobs such as clerical and class IV positions compared to members of forward Hindu and Christian communities who occupy managerial or professional positions. The general picture of the conditions of the Muslim community as explained by the late Asgar Ali Engineer that 'the Muslims occupy a niche position characterised by self-employment in petty business/trade and tend to fall behind forward community—Hindus and Christians—in access to education and formal sector jobs is also true in the case of Muslims in Kerala'. In the analogy of Jeffrey and Jeffrey, "In the matter of employment, low and high, Muslims are sandwiched between forward Hindu community and Christians on the one hand and Dalits who lie at the bottom."

While communities/social classes with higher educational attainment tended to improve their socio-economic conditions, Muslims with lower attainment remain as low or under achievers. Lack of/low educational attainment combined with socio-economic difficulties rendered them powerless. The constraint in sharing power and resources with other communities perpetuated their marginalisation. Despite government efforts to improve the education level of the poor, disadvantaged, destitute sections, including backward minorities, their condition hardly improves. Because of the proportionately low level of participation in higher/professional education human capital formation (a process of increasing knowledge, skills and the capabilities of people) among the community is very weak, which impinges on their competency, empowerment and human development.

With the recent spurt in educational participation, although the educational attainment among Muslims has improved significantly during the last decade, it has not expanded widely to benefit the community horizontally. There has been wide concern that the poor disadvantaged Muslim students are "not doing well" in schools, especially in rural areas where those who qualify for higher education are few in number. These "not doing well" section of students eventually tend to dropout. The school dropout having little liking for knowledge wander idly and aimlessly through the streets or are invariably reduced to running errands in market places.

The fact of the persistent high rate of failures and dropouts (non-completion of courses) among the disadvantaged sections of the community signifies digress in the community's education attainment levels. Even today, their low educational attainment continues to be one of the major issues in the performance of their human and social development.

The community's stock of educational attainment continues to be marginal. The level of capability enhancement of large proportion of its members is not so encouraging, when compared to that being achieved by other social classes.

To improve this situation, high quality public controlled, inclusive education, good quality government schools especially for Muslim girls are suggested.[16]

In Kerala the Muslim population, now generally well conscious of the importance of educating their children, shows very much eagerness to improve their education level. At present education, a foundation for continued advance is a high priority among a large section of the members of the Muslim community. The awakening that in order to advance in the society along with other communities needs better education encourages community members in this matter. Contrary to the perception that low returns from education deters parents from encouraging their children to pursue education, especially higher education, the present generation of parents give more importance to education irrespective of the level of likely returns.

It is to be noted that 92 per cent respondents affirmed that non-availability of appropriate employment opportunities on the basis of educational qualification is not a discouragement in giving education to their children. But for 88 per cent, the belief that those who attain higher education qualification will get employment that yields low income is not a factor that deters the parents from giving higher education to their children. Only a minority of 12 per cent consider income as a factor while sending their wards for higher education.

Conclusion

Evidences from micro level experience suggest that numerous factors like family income and parental education, future ambitions, value perceptions of parents, religious obsession and orthodoxy, influence and teachings of a section of the clergy who discourage women from going out of their homes, presently rising education consciousness or absence of it and the new found identity determine education decisions of Muslim households.

Still iniquitous distribution of education service and the unbearable cost of providing higher education impinge on the education attainment of the less privileged section of the Muslim community and is a detracting element in the education of their children. That the "Muslims do not see education as necessarily translating into formal employment" and that "the low representation of Muslims in public or private sector employment and the perception of discrimination in securing salaried jobs" make them give less importance to formal 'secular education' is true to a great extent in the case of less educated, tradition bound orthodox Muslims in some parts of Kerala. Despite significant progress in the education sector in contemporary Kerala, the education 'stocks'[17] (education attainment levels) of the Muslim community is short of the desired levels.

Notwithstanding difficulties, the community presently shows much eagerness to advance education of their children. At present education, a foundation for continued progress, is a high priority among a large section of the members of the community.

Notes and References

1. *See* Janet R. Dickson *et al.*, (2010), *Advancing Global Education; Patterns of Potential Human Progress*, Vol.2, Oxford, New Delhi, p. 16
2. Government of India, 2006.

3. Asgar Ali Engineer (2001), *'Muslim Middle Class and its Role'*, Centre for Study of Society and Secularism, Mumbai.
4. Sonalde Desai and Veena Kulkarni (2010), Unequal Playing Field: Socio-Religious Inequalities in Educational Attainment, in Rakesh Basant and Abusaleh Shariff, *Hand Book of Muslims*, Oxford University Press, p. 273.
5. *Handbook of Muslims*, Oxford, New Delhi, p. 4.
6. Jean Dreze and Amartya Sen (1995), *'India: Economic Development and Social Opportunity'*, Oxford University Press, New Delhi.
7. Quoted from Farooqui (2002), in *Handbook of Muslims*, p. 190.
8. Sukhadeo Thorat and Katherine S. Newman, (Eds.) (2010), *Blocked by Economic Discrimination in Modern India*, Oxford, New Delhi, Chapters 8&9.
9. Sachar Committee Report, pp. 15-16.
10. *See Handbook of Muslims*, Oxford, New Delhi, p. 4.
11. Note the 'stock' of educational attainment of a community is an important indicator of its human capabilities.
12. Lloyd I Rudolph and Susanne Hoeber Rudolph (2008), *Regional Patterns of Education: Rimland and Heartland in Indian Education*, in Explaining Indian Democracy: A Fifty Years' Perspective – 1956-2006 –The Realm of the Public Sphere, Identity and Policy, Oxford University Press, New Delhi, New York, p. 65.
13. *Education For All, Global Monitoring Report*, 2011, UNESCO Publishing, (Highlights), p. 4.
14. *See* Vanik Borooah (2010), On the Risk of belonging to Disadvantaged Groups, in Rakesh Basant, Abusaleh Sharif, (Eds.) *Handbook of Muslims*, Oxford, pp. 211-213.
15. For an analogous discussion *see*, Janet R. Dickson *et al*., (2010) *Advancing Global Education: Patterns of Potential Human Progress* (Volume 2) Oxford University Press, New Delhi, p. 15.
16. *See* also Sachar Committee recommendations.
17. Note the 'stock' of educational attainment of a community is an important indicator of its human capabilities.

6

Privatisation of Education and Empowerment

Experience of the Muslim Community in Kerala

Empowerment of the backward and marginalised minority communities has been a priority element in the contemporary development policies of governments. Governments pursue the policy of development through social, economic and political empowerment of the weaker sections of the minority groups as a proper strategy. Among the various minorities, the need to empower the Muslim community, who had been subject to social, economic and political discrimination and neglect, and to exclusion from decision-making processes, is most pressing and urgent because large section of the community continues to be marginalised, helpless and abandoned, powerless, and less privileged. In fact, this task is very strenuous due to the complexity of the issues involved and the ever widening social and economic gap between forward – advanced communities and less advanced – backward minority communities. Inadequate opportunity for self-sufficiency, low self-confidence and self-reliance, inequality, inequity and dependence are hurdles in the path of empowerment of the minority communities. Society featuring structures of dominancy by privileged groups, hostile social attitude and irrational behaviour of other communities, oligarchic behaviour of administrative authorities and their unfavourable, discriminatory and unfair treatment adversely affect empowerment of the Muslim community.

Education system is expected to facilitate empowerment of the backward and unprivileged communities enabling them to gain power, access to resources, expansion of assets and capabilities, to assert choices, attain self-reliance, and to exercise greater control over their lives and well-being. The ability of people to exercise choice and control over their lives is critical. Marginalised people could be mainstreamed by increasing their self-confidence and self-respect and self-image.

Empowering the poor and backward minorities needs integrating themselves into the mainstream of the polity and economy, enabling them to participate efficaciously in social, political, economic and cultural processes so as to end their dependence, servility/servitude, and subordination. It also requires ending exercise of disproportionate power by the elite sections that dominate/control political organisations and institutions. That is, inequality/asymmetry in power relations needs to be redressed and socio-economic and political exclusion of minorities restricted.

Education has the core purpose of developing the youth with knowledge and equipping them with the skills they need to develop a secure livelihood and to participate in social, cultural, economic and political life, promoting inclusive growth that is recognised as central to the development agenda. Quite crucial it has been touted as a tool for empowerment of the less privileged.

Education when used as a weapon to change society enables communities to achieve social and economic mobility, and, progress and empowerment in life. When people are educated they become organized and attain resources to gain empowerment, and galvanize community's collective efforts to progress. And hence, education for empowerment has always been a core agenda of the government. For this objective to be achieved, educational institutions should be open and accessible equally to all sections of society. Public education must have the objective of empowering the poor, backward and disenfranchised to change their communities and improve their lives and societies[1] by gaining social-political, and economic power, becoming liberated economically and socially to pursue their welfare and change their social constructions. Popular education must be designed to ensure/encourage community engagement and social interaction, and integrate various classes of people together so that they attain strength and become powerful.

Nonetheless, private education institutions, owned and managed by pro-profit and non-profit agencies, are hugely outnumbering public institutions and the unreachability of the former category by the poor sections/communities, compound the problem of empowerment of the community. The problem has become much more complex, especially, in the context of globalization-privatisation and market orientation of education and the consequent paradigm shift in the development strategy and policies of governments. The disadvantaged sections among the people perceive privatisation of education as serving the upper elite class interests.

Here in this part, an investigation is undertaken to ascertain the impact of privatisation of education on the empowerment of the socially and economically backward Muslim community[2] in Kerala. The methodology adopted is predominantly empirical with a minor support of descriptive method. Empirical data yielded from a household survey conducted in four districts of the State viz. Malappuram, Palghat, Kannur and Trivandrum where a substantial portion of Muslim population is present. A sampling of 800 respondents (Muslim community), 200 from each district was selected on a random basis for the purpose. Care was taken to cover all categories of people in the community. Although, the researcher in no way makes any claim as to the sampling being representative of the entire Muslim community in the State.

The survey focused on the parameters within which empowerment of the powerless takes place. The prospects of education under privatised structure helping the powerless to acquire the necessary empowerment, by reducing socio-economic gap between different communities, removing backwardness etc. are probed. Nonetheless, the difficulty to directly observe the extent and efficiency with which the goals of privatisation of education policy are materialised is a limitation in this respect. It is not easy to determine the criteria for the success of the policy in terms of empowering the minority communities, who endure 'poverty in education'.

Privatisation of Education and Empowerment of the Backward Muslim Community in Kerala

The ideological underpinnings of globalization tend to treat education as an industry, which provides a service that should be traded. Education in this context has become a tradable and traded service which led to opening of the education system to large scale privatisation. It is explained as 'private provision of a public service', the government arranging for its people to receive education service without the government actually providing it directly. Neo-liberal globalisation and privatisation of education service is advocated in terms of quality improvement with provision for cost recovery. Academic capitalism defines education service delivery as a tradable one. The public sector education that was once responsible for providing universal education and protecting equality of opportunity is a veritable challenge. The rollback of public education under the weight of proliferation of private unaided schools and self-financing colleges is feared to render access to education of their choice quite difficult which is likely to result in inequality in education attainment.

The indiscriminate policy of granting recognition and affiliation to educational institutions has led to the virtual take-over of the education sector by profit and commercially oriented private managements. The resource and capacity deficits were constraints to look to the merits of the choice for or against privatisation. Without rationally evaluating the costs and benefits of direct provision of education service by government-run public institutions against the provision of the same by private institutions, the government allowed the latter a free run even to subject government's education policy to blackmail. Failure to execute binding agreements regarding obligations of the private institutions made matters worse. The government turning its function of education service over to private institutions without provision for monitoring, controlling or auditing, their performance left people without any means to hold the government accountable for policy failure. Under the circumstances, educational institutions are run as if they were business centres. Professional educational institutions, especially, are wedded to a functional market economy. Education has become a commercial venture. As in the case of trade and commerce, under private-sector education, money/wealth has occupied the centre-stage. Now those who want higher (professional) education must pay for it. Due to little spending by government on education, the entire financing responsibility shifts to parents/students.

Privatisation, turning market-oriented, market- dominated and profit- ownership of education, gradually replaces the values associated with traditional education and knowledge. In the new dispensation, where marketisation changes people's relations and values towards stimulating those of the market, educational practices became mere business practices and education is treated as a commodity. In this context private agencies running educational institutions, whether pro-profit or non-profit, always have their own prosperity at the top of their minds.

Privatisation of education programme in the state has certainly led to expansion of educational facilities and opportunities, usually viewed as the most potent tool to address the problems of inequalities, and contributed to improvement in enrolment of members of backward minority communities not only in primary and secondary education but also in tertiary education across the State, including backward and hitherto neglected Malabar region, which was for long educationally backward and where Muslim community is largely present.

Muslim children gained opportunities to pursue and complete education, including higher studies and a section of the Muslim community has advanced its educational status. However, although massive expansion of education facilities has the objective to generate and disseminate knowledge and provide easy access to education to the common people, under the present system, it is the well-off who have easy access to private institutions and who increasingly use the opportunity they provide for higher education. Only the wealthy, economically and educationally privileged upper, middle and higher classes in the society can afford the exorbitant expenses of higher professional education and gain benefits. For persons without hefty financial resources, access to education provided by private institutions remains a dream too hard to realise.

Most private investment in higher education is concentrated in professional education sector, and great majority of such private sector institutions are 'surrogate businesses' which use surreptitious practices in admission of students, and charge exorbitantly high fees. Even those under cooperative sector are no exception. Rapid expansion of private medical and engineering institutions have given a further impetus to the menace of capitation fees unbearable to average parents. Parents have to part with hefty amounts in astronomic proportions between the ranges of 50 to 90 lakhs to get admission in a private medical college.

Tuition fee and private spending have been steeply increasing. Few children of poor parents can bear the exorbitant and arbitrary non-fee costs of the private educational institutions, including schools. Parents have to overspend to get their children entry into such private institutions and pursue education.

Private sector delivering education service can be an empowerment tool if transparency in its management is ensured, per student cost is low and affordable to the poor, marginalised communities, and if equity considerations receive priority. But, lack of transparency, higher cost of education including prohibitively higher fees in private sector has tended to drive the poor, disadvantaged backward minority students, out of the system, and to reduce educational attainment among the poor members of the Muslim community.

Despite policy averment that the principle of equity and social justice will guide the provision of education by private institutions, not everything is transparent and fair in regard to admission of students to private institutions. That their managements resort to dubious practices is apparent from many of their actions like opposition to admitting students from the rank list prepared by the State Entrance Commissioner or a test conducted under the supervision of the Admission Supervisory Committee (ASC).

Although the private education institutions are defined non-profit institutions, the reality of capitation and high tuition fees they collect disproves the claim. The element of profiteering is very much apparent in private education system in the State. Many of the private agencies that obtained permission to start and manage professional colleges in the State have profit-making motive, and are of doubtful credentials. Many of them are profit corporations, devoid of any of the past tradition of philanthropic principles. They tend to take control of education along with other public services such as health care, previously delivered by the government. In fact, private provision of education slowly but certainly brings about a fundamental transformation in the relationship between the government and people where the latter appear powerless to compel/influence the government to deliver affordable education to their children. The consequence of this phenomenon is imbalances in the higher education attainment across various socio-economic groups, defeat of equality of opportunity and inclusiveness in education, distorting the concept of social advancement of the socially backward and poor, and negating the goals of social justice.

A large majority of respondents (80 per cent) asserted that privatisation of education has resulted in virtual commercialisation of education rendering education unaffordable and inaccessible to the less advantaged sections of the minority communities, especially the backward and poor sections. A great majority of 75 per cent respondents testified that private self-financing educational institutions are meant only for higher categories of people in society. It is a small section of higher economic status and influence who can afford money to pay for their education and manage to get entry into coveted, high status and high paid jobs. That accessibility to education under private sector is limited to the privileged sections has been endorsed by majority of respondents.

- In a sense, capitalist commercial interest in private sector education tends to serve privilege. Private education institutions have become the exclusive domain of 'the forces of privilege', and are divorced from students of poor, disadvantaged, and marginalised sections of the society. Wealthy parents use the system to suit their purposes of extraction of education degrees/diplomas to their children. Having an edge in gaining entry in elite private institutions irrespective of their academic ability, they increasingly and almost invariably benefit disproportionately from the expansion of private education institutions.
- The private sector, even that is under the "Muslim managements" lacks transparency and is hardly sensitised to the plight of the poor and disadvantaged sections of the community. In such conditions only limited educational opportunities are accessible to the less privileged. As Amartya Sen says under this system, "right to higher education is the right of the educationally privileged to study further at the expense of the society irrespective of one's academic ability....."[3] The tradition of private educational institutions being run on philanthropic principles has dwindled. These institutions today are not socially inclusive. The basic structure of the present

education system as distorted by privatisation and its narrow petty objectives of profit has been higher-privileged class biased and elite-friendly. 'Public good' nature of education and its non-profit character are challenged.

Under-privileged parents and children struggle to obtain education of their choice which is discriminately denied to them as an individual entitlement just because of lack of their purchasing capacity. Majority of students who have poor socio-economic background and who cannot access privatised higher education benefit little from this system and are not successful in capability development. The private-self-financed educational institutions hardly respond to the needs of the poor. The elitist, commercial class bias in the privatisation policy, and its emphasis on economic criterion for gaining accessibility to education shatters equity in education. This education policy is diametrically opposed to the age-long notions about the nature and functions of public education. Its exclusivist nature has elements of disempowerment of the disadvantaged and underprivileged sections of the people. It barely helps socio-economic mobility of the poor within the community. This certainly affects empowerment of the unprivileged sections in the society in general, and the section within the minority Muslim community in particular.

Unbridled proliferation of unaided private English medium schools in the recent past, and the steady increase in enrolment in such schools in Kerala have led to a steady fall in enrolment in private-aided and government schools. A competitive atmosphere has come to define the education sector which resulted in 'uneconomic schools' which face threat of closure. It is to be noted that majority of poor and lower class children enrol in government or private-aided schools and other higher institutions. This 'un economy' syndrome makes privatisation a concern for both learners as well as teachers alike.

With improvement in general enrolment, although enrolment of minorities has also improved, disparities between different classes persist. Inter-community and intra-community disparities in terms of education between advanced and marginalised sections which include large sections of Muslim community are still high. Whereas the completion of graduation and higher level of education by members of a community determines its educational attainment, the share of graduates and higher degree holders in the Muslim community, especially the young, in fact, is less than that of other forward communities, even less than that of the general population share. In effect, the Muslim community in Kerala suffers from a "deficit" in education participation and attainment, compared with other forward communities. In general, Muslim participation in education, especially in higher/ professional science and technology and management education is lower than that of other sections of the population. And, in fact, the community is underrepresented in professional education.

Access and Equity Problems

Issues of access and equity are central to the education debates everywhere. But the growing private share in education in Kerala has its own bearing on access and equity. Perhaps, exact goals of the privatisation policy have not been explicitly stated in broad terms, except mention of preventing student outflow to neighbouring states.

Conditions of private educational institutions generate inequalities and affect adversely the empowerment of the poor. Denial of access to educational opportunities of their choice to the students just because they have no capacity to meet the expenses of education led to an increase in inequalities and iniquity within the community.

Facilities and learning environment are not equal in all institutions. In this respect some institutions can be treated as more equal than others. In wealthier institutions facilities are disproportionately large. Students in poor institutions, especially schools, have less access to educational infrastructure. And poor students with financial difficulties are pitted against wealthy students. In general, an economically disadvantageous environment exists vis-a-vis poor minority students who are predominantly in the public education sphere in the State. Particularly in public schools, negligence in advanced infrastructure facilities and failure in supply of books on time result in their underachievement in acquiring advanced knowledge which is acknowledged as part of a universal right to education. School inequality adversely affects advancement of education of poor minority students. This system not only accelerates inequalities in learning attainments and widen existing social gaps, but also perpetuates injustice. And private educators contribute to the creation of larger social gap between the rich and the poor. It is obvious that injustice and inequality are embedded in the private education system. Poor (minority) students account for the worst sufferers. In this system of discrepancy since equal education does not exist, it is difficult to ensure education for all children.

The large iniquities in terms of socio-economic inequalities, lower participation of the poor in education and the socio-economic dominance and uneven privileges some segments endure, in fact, impede ability of the poor in taking advantage of educational opportunities (viewed as the most potent tool to overcome backwardness and inequalities) thrown open by expansion of educational institutions under private sector.

Despite some impressive gains in regard to enrolment and completion of education, the stark feature of the present system of education is widening of inequality between the privileged and less privileged. Perhaps, there is a surge in inequality within the community as well as between communities posing a major obstacle to equitable development and empowerment of the backward communities, including the backward minorities.

In fact, the effect of private provision of education (as public service) in the long run will be far reaching. Weakening of common education system and inexorably rising inequality in educational attainment will lead to further marginalisation of the less privileged sections among the minority communities – a disempowering experience.

Government's policy of privatisation of education has not been helpful to fill the education gap (also knowledge and technology gap) because it was not inclusive or equitable and could not ensure better education for the backward and poor among the minorities

Although creation of educational facilities under private sector opens opportunities for backward segments in the minority groups, empirical evidence shows that lack of ability to pay for private education, the real cost of which is sharply high, keeps them out of the realm. Since attainment of higher education perhaps is linked to wealth and other social and economic privileges, only the rich are in advantageous position to complete the same. Poor Muslim students who complete secondary education, the corner stone of education, although have the same chance as that of the forward communities and advanced sections in pursuing Tertiary education, cannot pursue an education of their choice because of disadvantages associated with low economic status and other factors.

Community disparity in tertiary enrolment is too wide as the rich and forward sections are more successful in securing higher enrolment. As access to tertiary education expands in the case of the rich households whose rate of completion of higher education is high, inequalities in skill development also increase.

With regard to the question of privatisation helping children of backward minority communities attain full and equal access to and achievement in basic education of good quality, the response was mixed. Empirical evidence shows that, despite being eligible, the economically and socially backward children among the minority Muslim community hardly succeed in securing access/admission to private-unaided educational institutions, because of their inability to afford higher fees and due to lack of affordable institutions. In fact, privatisation policy places severe limitations on the backward children's meaningful choices and puts a high premium on their access to education and empowerment.

Economically and socially backward and disadvantaged children encounter a system in which the children of elite, upper class affluent parents, though are dumb and of poor academic score, are fortunate to pursue their education in good, well-financed public schools/colleges or private ones and manage to secure higher degrees/diplomas, while the less advantaged/marginalised ones, though are with high academic score, get a far poor education, or abandon their ambition for higher education. In regard to the less privileged sections, ability and possibility to provide quality education and possibility to decide on the kind of education to be given to their children is hindered. This system engenders in-egalitarian social conditions and acts against the principles of redistribution of resources (education as essential human resource).

Because of different types of school education under the system, children of different sections of society acquire varying quality of education in accordance with their socio-economic and cultural status/purchasing capacity. Elite schools cream-off the economically well-off students while the poor having no choice are left out to struggle in 'sink' schools. A vast gap of resources, facilities and efficiency that exists between well-run private schools and colleges which cater for the better-off strata of society and the ones run by the government can be noted.[4] Inequalities are implied in the system. In fact, a hierarchical system of education service provision, resulting from its increasing privatisation causes and perpetuates wide inequality in education achievement among different strata of society and reinforces class-based privileges.

Too many educational institutions under private sector majorly undertaking responsibility of education service delivery left government and government-aided education institutions insignificant. Quality of public education service received by the less advantaged sections suffers. In fact, there is considerable variation in quality of varied types of educational institutions which serve different socio-economic groups differently. It produces incompetence and sharpens the existing inequalities in education of the poor and has only minimal scope of enhancing their welfare and empowerment. Also, the provision of education service by private institutions would hardly make the disadvantaged communities powerful.

In the context of the general criticism that it is the higher strata of the society and the middle classes who enjoy disproportionate benefits of privatisation, public perception on this aspect was sought in the survey. The survey results predominantly confirmed the criticism as 82 per cent of the respondents affirmed this.

Expansion of educational institutions under unaided-private sector could hardly help in solving the issue of access disparity and poor academic capability/attainment (academic score) of the Muslim community. These features, in fact, tend to widen intra-community and inter-community disparities which are worrying and embarrassing, and are not helpful for community empowerment. The outcome of widening learning disparities between rich and poor students, especially of minority communities is not conducive for inculcating ideal social relations to construct shared values that enrich and transform communities.

Scope of Private Sector Education as a Tool of Empowerment

Public perception regarding privatisation of education helping education of poor Muslims

Data Analysis

Public perception on the question of increase in private educational institutions helping education of the poor among the Muslim community was sought in the survey conducted among sampling households in four districts in the state. 54 per cent of the respondents asserted that increase in private educational institutions has not been helpful for the education of the poor among the Muslim community, whereas 46 per cent held the view that privatisation benefits the community including the poor sections. In the perception of a good majority (67 per cent) of respondents 'establishment of increasing number of private self-financing educational institutions has not been helpful for the educational progress of the Muslim community as such; although, however, 33 per cent saw helpful impact.

In the Muslim community, there is significant increase in the number of persons with higher education, graduate and professional qualification, but the community as such has not yet been able to improve their educational status to the extent of other social groups such as forward Hindu and Christian communities. The community's education stock has not substantially improved so as to enable it to access and control resources as an entitlement. Private education providers do little to promote education among the backward minority communities, nor at least to minimally meet their education needs. Due to the relatively poor 'stock' of educational attainment, the community has not been able to improve its human capability and effectively influence or control government policy making to its advantage as the other communities do.

The views of respondents in this respect are almost even divided. It is not safe to assert that privatisation does not benefit the people at all or that people do not make use of it. Privatisation benefits people, but predominantly the higher class has an edge in making use of it. In this circumstance, we must conclude that mere expansion of institutions under private sector will not make education inclusive to benefit all sections of the society unless barriers to access education are removed.

Although it is gratifying to note a majority of 53 per cent respondents affirming that Muslim students have opportunities similar to students from other communities in the case of admission to private self-financing educational institutions, the view of a considerable section of 47 per cent that Muslim students do not get the same opportunities availed by non-Muslim students is a matter of much concern.

With regard to the matter of securing admission and studying in private self-financing medical/engineering colleges, 53 per cent respondents viewed that Muslim students get opportunities similar to that are available to students of other communities while a significant portion of respondents (47 per cent) considered it inaccurate.

77 per cent of the household respondents view that the opportunity to receive professional education is not equally open to all communities, while 23 per cent had the alternate view. What this implies is that opportunities available to all are not equally accessible to all. Hence, it is difficult for all sections of the population to make use of the opportunities, although they are available equally.

Observation of 62 per cent of respondents shows that 'all students of the Muslim community do not make use of the opportunities to study in the self-financing educational institutions, whereas for 38 per cent, all of them avail such opportunities. In fact, it is obvious that only a minority makes use of the opportunities, thrown open by private self-financing educational institutions. Of the respondents interviewed, 99 per cent did not avail themselves of bank loan for educational purposes. This does not mean that people have no need for financial assistance to meet educational expenses.

Parents, who invest in their children's education, push them to join professional courses expecting returns. With this objective, and ready to go to any length, they invest in children's education even mortgaging properties or availing loans and end up in indebtedness and consequent debt woes and remain depressed with burdens–a disempowering phenomenon. But dependence on bank loan for educational purposes is risky because of the uncertainty regarding the students' employment prospects after completion of education. A large number of students who took huge education loans from banks did not find suitable jobs after studies to repay the loans, and remain frustrated and distressed. For the economically weaker among them the burden of interest on the principal of the loan and penal interest for defaulting on repayment is very daunting. A dreadful crisis builds up in the education loan sector. Nonetheless, majority of respondents (89 per cent) held the view that pursuing higher education by utilising educational loans from banks was useful. Their observation shows that a few, though not substantial number of the poor and backward community students makes use of Bank loans for educational purposes. Yet 75 per cent of the respondents are of the view that poor and backward sections of the Muslim community have difficulties in getting educational loans from the banks.

Reducing Socio-economic Gap

Data Analysis

- Public perception on the suitability of the prevailing education system to reduce the social-economic gap between different communities, essential for empowerment of the weaker sections, remains divided. In the survey, 60 per cent of the respondents affirmed the suitability of the prevailing education system to reduce the gap, while 40 per cent underlined its unsuitability. 84 per cent of the respondents endorsed the view that the present system of education is helpful in bringing about social change and progress in society. 73 per cent of respondents believe that modern system of education provides the right type of education helpful to remove the backwardness of the Muslim community, and 74 per cent believe that it is helpful in liberating the new generation from their servitude to individuals and ideologies. This certainly does not reflect the general perception of the people as a whole. Elite sections differ from the views of the ordinary respondents as 72 per cent of them expressed contrary views and asserted that the present system of education will not reduce inequalities. Left-oriented intellectuals, leaders and teachers, 89 per cent of them interviewed, also concur with this view.
- A great majority of respondents (73 per cent) found that earning degrees after paying high fees will create inequality in society. Only a minority (27 per cent) have different perception.
- According to 83 per cent respondents, Muslim students will not get extra consideration and care other than that are received by non-Muslim students in educational institutions managed/ controlled by Muslim community groups or individuals, although in the perception of 17 per cent respondents, extra

care and consideration for Muslim students in such institutions are possible.

- Somewhat comforting is the affirmation by 66 per cent of the respondents that Muslim students do not experience any inconvenience or difficulties or discrimination in schools and colleges controlled by non-Muslim communities or individuals, although 34 per cent respondents felt otherwise.

The above two majority views are influenced by the commercial character of education service by private institutions, which provide education as a tradable service for profit, and hence, all service recipients are alike.

Since a majority of educational institutions are owned and managed by powerful religious/community groups, backward minorities who are not able to establish and manage sufficient number of educational institutions proportionate to their needs are left behind the powerful communities in the matter of educational achievement. While an unequal and iniquitous pattern of privatisation has been reinforced without addressing the issue of narrowing the intercommunity and intra community divides in opportunity for education, especially for higher and professional education, individual achievements, community progress and empowerment are hindered. Moreover, no significant improvement takes place in the status of these 'education disadvantages' of the poor sections of the minorities.

Furthermore, under the policy of globalisation-liberalisation induced privatisation affirmative actions hitherto pursued to correct historical social-economic imbalances, injustice and discrimination are difficult.

Improvement in Economic Status

- Despite expansion of education due to privatisation, Muslim individuals' relative disadvantage vis-a-vis members of forward communities in accessing quality education impinges on their ability to gain substantive economic advantages. It is true that a large number of individuals from the Muslim community who managed to acquire basic education and new technical skills and complete professional education gained employment reaping the benefits of the surging developments. They contribute to improvement in the economic status of their households. Nonetheless, the system has contributed not equality of opportunity because of the linking of entry/ admission to private institutions to economic ability/ status. It is a very small advanced section that benefits from private institutions and manages to get access to high status and best paid jobs and further improves their socio-economic status. Economic disadvantages prevent poor minority students from making use of educational opportunities opened by privatisation. For a number of Muslim graduates, education is not fully transforming into formal higher income yielding employment. Except a few members of urban-based upper middle class sections, very few among the educated Muslims are employed in high income, high dignity and privileged positions in high profile public or corporate sector. In educated Muslim community, there is no significant breakthrough among the members improving their economic status by gaining entry into coveted regular jobs or improving productivity and incomes in self-employment.

Data Analysis

According to 62 per cent of the respondents, all students who acquire degrees from self-financing sector do not secure dignified and deserving employment, although, 38 per cent confirmed such possibility. With the expansion of higher education, problem of unemployment and underemployment of graduates also tends to grow. The ubiquitous new generation private self-financing professional colleges do seldom assure the graduates a career with dignity, self-respect and decent salaries.

Majority of ordinary graduates that the system produces actually end up in jobs that do not require graduate skills and have to live with low status jobs and small salaries and remain dejected. It is also becoming obvious that a great number of the graduates churned out by the system are unfit for new jobs being created in the global market or have no employable/marketable skills. This phenomenon slaps on the self-esteem and dignity of the poor graduates and creates a sense of powerlessness among them.

According to 61 per cent respondents, those who earn degrees from private institutions, although, are able to start self-employment programmes, remain idle because of lack of resources and confidence. A significant section of respondents (39 per cent) were not optimistic in this matter.

Although a few Muslim community members who have educational attainment enter into private/corporate sector jobs, access to high prestige jobs is still a dream for many of them whereas large number of candidates belonging to forward community parents access such jobs or enter into employment in schools and colleges run by their communities than a Muslim candidate for whom such avenues are too limited. The 'cultural capital' reflected in parents' education level of the forward community candidates helps and increases their children's chances of gaining higher education and access to high prestige jobs whereas the Muslim parents and their children are at a drawback in this matter. Muslim members' pastures yield inferior outcomes. The poor Muslim students benefit only insignificant gains from privatisation of education even where educational institutions are managed by Muslim individuals, although, Muslim parents predominantly showed inclination to send their children to institutions run by Muslim management.

Quality Decline in Education

Data Analysis

In the perception of 54 per cent respondents, the private self-financing education system will not ensure complete and equal quality education to all students, although 46 per cent believe that private institutions have the commitment to ensure quality education to all students. The truth is that success rate of private self-financing professional institutions is woefully low, that is below 40 per cent and in some cases even below 20 per cent. Only a small number of students who secure entry into private self-financing institutions manage to pass the examination worthily. A great majority of those who fail end up in low status jobs and hardly achieve other elements of empowerment.

While 64 per cent of respondents viewed the present system of privatisation defined by self-financing of cost of education as appropriate to fulfil the learning needs of the student community, 36 per cent denied the possibility. Yet privatisation and lack of rational planning in education have the consequence of over education/excess training in certain areas leaving many graduates unemployed or underemployed for long and hindering scope for empowerment.

70 per cent of respondents have confirmed that privatisation/ commercialisation of education has set out to destroy/sacrifice the lofty objectives and values of education while 30 per cent of the respondents denied such negative effect. Freewheeling private enterprises running educational institutions with 'business expectations'/capitalist greed, using 'business methods' tends to destroy public education values/ objectives such as equity, equality, human dignity, social cohesion etc. The system being exploited by a privileged section is responsible for youth discontent and depression which tend to grow.

The Community Advancing Towards Progress and Empowerment

The educated must redistribute and exchange knowledge and develop common cause with others, particularly fellow community members. They must work to bring about social change by 'building truthful, lasting, joyful relationships among fellow beings to transform self-efficacy to collective efficacy, strive for collective survival by accessing government and other community resources and achieve better control over the environment and decision-making. They should function effectively in society, contribute to collective social and community actions accessing collective power, authority and influence, and be facilitators of empowerment. In an educated community, different groups could get together to contribute to community development, individual ability contributing to community potential and to joint goals of empowerment of the community. Hence, Muslim students who study in high fee charging private self-financing educational institutions, while achieving individual ability and self-development are believed to contribute to the development of the Muslim community as well. As the Quran emphasises, they must act righteously, reflected in a social behaviour of cooperation for the common good and progress. They must develop individual and collective obligations that are mutually complementary, the outcome of such behaviour benefitting the community/society as a whole. Views of the public with regard to this aspect as ascertained from the survey are analysed here.

Data Analysis

Table 5(a): Views of the public regarding Muslim students studying in high fee charging private self-financing education institutions while achieving self-development also contributing to the development of the Muslim community

Contribute to develop the Muslim community	*Contribute to some extent*	*Do not contribute*	*Lack any understanding on this issue.*
31 per cent	12 per cent	20 per cent	37 per cent

In terms of students of private educational institutions acquiring self-efficacy, self-esteem, competency, locus of control, which are crucial to empowerment of individuals and transformation from a passive situation to an active situation of control over factors that affect life, the record of Muslim community members is only moderate.

The survey result confirms that progress in self-efficacy and individual ability does not largely transform into collective efficacy/community potential. The individual development does not largely result in sustainable and stable community development. Under privatisation, education being commercialised, advantaged groups are reinforced in their pursuit of narrow self-interest, with little empathy with the poor. The education the groups gain and the intellect and skills they develop are not substantially used to address the numerous problems the community faces. Individual empowerment does not significantly transform into community empowerment. Community empowerment is hardly an agenda of the sector. Under private sector education, community development/empowerment orientation is being divested of. Commercialisation of education is presumed to be the reason for this. Education of an individual that depends on the basis of the thickness of his purse atomizes rather than build community. The community as such could not attain the necessary wherewithal to gain control over its forward and upward mobility in the socio economic and political sphere. In fact, individual ability transforming into community potential, contributing to community's economic power and empowerment, the record of the Muslim community is unappreciable.

68 per cent of the respondents testified that establishment of self-financing professional educational institutions – medical, engineering – under private sector, has not helped to remove the backwardness of the Muslim community as such while the perception of 32 per cent was in the positive direction. It is few individuals who benefit and improve their socio-economic status. Nonetheless, individual benefits barely transform into community benefits. In the perception of 64 per cent respondents this has not helped the empowerment of the Muslim community, but for 36 per cent, the community gained empowerment to some extent. According to 58 per cent respondents, these institutions are neither helpful to ensure equal justice to all sections of the population in society although 24 per cent recorded their views in the affirmative sense. It is an irony that 18 per cent respondents remain without understanding of the private institutions delivering justice to different sections of people in the society.

- Further 58 per cent of the respondents held the view that students who pursue their education after giving higher fees in private institutions lead a lifestyle different from that of the civil society, although 42 per cent observed little difference in lifestyle. Perhaps, the majority view students studying in high fee charging private educational institutions later tend to separate themselves from the civil society to lead particular type of lifestyle. Such students, according to 85 per cent respondents are too focused on their personal achievements.
- Even social relations and inter-personal equations are sought to be defined in terms of resources. Dowry and related marriage expenses, particularly among those educated under private institutions, meeting high cost of education, showing ugly and wanton ostentatious display of wealth, vanity, pomp and splendour and hard bargaining for material assets, create social problems. Unhealthy practices abound on the arrangements of

marriages. Even educated and employed girls find hard to get along with this situation. This culture is not an enabling element that contributes towards community empowerment, but tends to disempower poor families. Although for a minority of respondents such students contribute and commit themselves to the progress of the society/community.

Privatisation is believed to be helpful to the common good of the society. However, public perception of this aspect is splintered.

Table 5(b) : Public perception with regard to privatisation of education helping to ensure common good of the society.

Privatisation of education is helpful to ensure common good of society	*Not helpful*	*Not sure/not aware of*
42 per cent	47 per cent	11 per cent

– Some scholars and even theorists may propose that the interest of the higher strata and middle classes are in congruent with the common interest of the society/ community. In the survey, while only a minority of 32 per cent of the respondents agreed with the proposition, a majority of 68 per cent argued against this view and insisted that the interest of the higher strata and the middle class are not in synergy with the common interest of the society/community.

Capacity to Self-Determine Lives

Individuals attaining capacity to self-determine their lives, without depending on others, and exerting influence in social, economic and political fields to bring about necessary changes to their advantages are important factors that count in empowerment. The views of respondents on these aspects were sought in the survey. 80 per cent of them affirmed that the present education system does not help students to self-determine their lives. Just 20 per cent have contrary view. According to 51 per cent those who acquire education under self-financing stream cannot take necessary decisions by themselves and without depending on others with regard to their growth and development, although a near percentage expressed in the positive.

According to 74 per cent of the respondents those who acquire education from private self-financing system can exert influence in social, economic and political fields and get them changed to their advantage. In this question just 24 per cent took negative view.

In the survey perception of respondents regarding all the persons who acquire medical/engineering education from self-financing institutions becoming capable in social, economic and political fields was sought. Their responses are categorised.

Table 5(c): Perception of respondents regarding medical/engineering graduates from private institutions becoming capable in socio-economic and political affairs.

Become capable	*Do not become capable*	*Unaware of the impact*
48 per cent	42 per cent	10 per cent

The views of respondents on the ability of professionally qualified persons to exert pressure on the employers and government to formulate and implement policies in their favour were sought. Their perceptions are categorised in Table 5(d).

Table 5(d): Views of respondents regarding ability of professionally qualified persons to exert pressure on government

Able to exert pressure	*Not able*	*No understanding of this matter*
49 per cent	33 per cent	18 per cent

Employer discretion to pick and choose, retain and retrench workers curtails worker freedom and bargaining power. Lack of scope for organisational network also hinders worker power putting a premium on their exerting pressure on government/employer.

Respondents were asked about medical/engineering graduates working under other employers according to their dictates developing their personality. Their response is categorised here.

Members of backward minority communities achieving upward mobility to reach the level of members of forward communities, through their educational achievement, is an essential requirement towards the empowerment of the former. The observation of respondents on this matter as ascertained from the survey is categorised in Table 5(f).

Table 5(e): Perception of respondents regarding the issue of medical/engineering graduates developing personality.

Develop personality	*Not develop*	*Not able to understand this fact*
24 per cent	56 per cent	20 per cent

Table 5(f): Observation of respondents regarding the members of Muslim community rising to the level of members of forward communities.

Individual members of the Muslim community could rise to the level of members of forward communities	*Poor sections among the community could not rise to the level*	*Not sure*
52 per cent	30 per cent	18 per cent

Members of backward minority communities with professional qualification working in private companies and other corporate sector leading self-reliant life is an important element that determines their empowerment. Observation of respondents on this matter is categorised.

Table 5(g) : Observation of respondents regarding members of Muslim community with professional qualifications working in private/corporate sector attaining/leading self-reliant life.

Attain/lead self-reliant life	*Do not attain/lead*	*Not sure*
57 per cent	34 per cent	9 per cent

Since most of the private investments in the field of education are in the areas of Engineering, Medicine and Management which require huge investment for education, benefits of large scale privatisation of provision of education in these sectors do not accrue for the underprivileged communities, including backward minority communities because the heavy burden of costs of education falls on them. Nor could they attain economic success or opportunities for upward mobility. The private providers do little to develop educational status of the backward communities. Delivery of educational service by private operators with narrow petty objectives of profit can hardly help the poor members of the minority Muslim community grow in stature and the nation prosper.

The present pattern of professional education oriented to the workforce requirements of industries has only nominal element of empowerment of the underprivileged community members who graduate in those professional fields. Expansion of professional education under private sector is to meet the market demands for labour with specific skills. Not all the graduates are appropriately equipped in skills required in job markets. There is a great mismatch between the skills, competency and know-how imparted on graduates of a large number of private professional educational institutions as reflected in many graduates in the areas of engineering, medicine and management are able to find only low profile, low paying jobs, or no jobs at all. The scope of such graduates getting empowered is limited. In fact, privatisation impedes community empowerment. Perhaps, education in the privatisation ambience tends to distort the empowerment agenda.

- Respondents overwhelmingly (99 per cent) believe that the Muslim students who have no economic means/ capacity to study in private self-financing institutions after giving high fees will be discontent and unrestful. The weaker sections who find it difficult to access to and do not benefit from the system remain dejected. That is, uunequal access to education opportunities under privatised conditions tending to generate frustration and sense of injustice among the younger folk is feared to trigger reactions/tension impinging on their chances of empowerment.
- This situation is not conducive for the growth and development of the community. However, according to 65 per cent of respondents, the above factor will not impede empowerment of the community as a whole, because empowerment is affected by many other factors as well. Although 35 per cent felt that the situation described above will impede empowerment.

Preference for Private Institutions

Despite the stark features of privatised pattern of education and the private sector institutions being alleged to be indulging in deceptive practices and misrepresentation of facts regarding their academic performance, preference for private educational institutions for education of children among the Muslim community, including the poor segments, is significant. It is because private institutions are believed to be intrinsically more likely to adapt to meet the needs of students. Parents are under the impression that all private institutions impart superior education. Lower levels of public educational institution performance, concerns over decline in public education quality, varying quality of institutions etc. deter parents from sending their children to such institutions. Concerns over discriminatory treatment, teacher complacency and unhelpful teacher attitude in public institutions force many parents to send their children to private sector education institutions although it imposes considerable financial burden on poor households. 65 per cent of the respondents affirmed that quality of education has improved due to privatisation and commercialisation of education, although 35 per cent has disagreed with this view.

Ordinary people, not well-informed, are not able to grasp the issues and problems and outcomes of self-financing system.

Conclusion

The test of an education system is whether it (a) promotes or thwarts full personal development, (b) accentuates or reduces inequality, (c) fulfils its core purpose of equipping the youth with the skills they need to develop a secure livelihood and to participate in social, economic and political life, (d) enables groups of people/ communities to achieve social and economic mobility and progress and empowerment in life, helping them acquire ability to enhance their self-reliance to assert their right to make choices, to control resources, to challenge and eliminate relations of domination and fight against their subordination.

Education system in Kerala has undergone drastic changes since the mid-1980s, and there is too wide privatisation in the sector, the state rolling back from the policy of defraying the cost of education service. Under the system the cost of education has increased exorbitantly, the burden falling on the students, despite the averred government declaration for the principle of equity and social justice to guide the policy.

Privatisation programme has certainly led to spread of education facilities across the State of Kerala, including backward and hitherto neglected areas where Muslim community is largely present. This enabled more and more Muslim students to pursue higher studies. Nonetheless, performance of the privatised liberal education system in the State towards the realisation of the lofty goals of education has been faulty. Profiteering and charging of capitation fee by private sector institutions being rampant, the principle of equity and justice and empowerment of the disadvantaged sections suffer a beating.

Public perception on the issue of the people in general benefitting from expansion of private educational institutions as ascertained from household survey remains more or less even divided. It is not safe to assert that privatisation is not totally beneficial or that all that is private is bad or that people do not make use of education opportunities thrown open by private sector. Privatisation benefits people, but predominantly the higher class who have an edge on making use of it.

Large scale privatisation of provision of education does not beneficially accrue for the underprivileged communities, including backward minority communities because the opportunity to receive education is not equally open to all communities. The issue of access disparity persists. Exorbitant higher per student cost under private sector drives the less privileged students out of the system. In fact, the system has led to denial of education to the economically and socially backward and marginalised among the minority Muslim community who find difficult to access education under private sector, although they have higher academic score and potential. As a result there is dramatic variance in educational (especially higher and professional level) attainment of different sections of people. Educational goals of poor Muslim community members remain unrealised or partially realised due to lack of ability to accomplish them. The under-representation/lower participation of Muslim candidates in higher professional education is proof of the exclusivist nature of private provision of education. Government intervention to address education backwardness and inequality among disadvantaged social groups through large extent of private provision of education, in fact, facilitated growth of exclusive privileges. The education participation rates of Muslim children and the education attainment levels of Muslim elders in Kerala continue to be relatively poor, despite the plan thrust on addressing the higher education needs of the hitherto excluded and under-represented groups including minorities. On the other hand, growth of education in other socio-religious communities tends to outpace the education growth among the Muslims, whose level of overall educational attainment is low.

The pace of advance and attainment in education has been uneven within the community, and the less privileged Muslim individuals though have opportunities are not able to use them and are unable to successfully complete higher level of education attainment and hence are further marginalised and excluded. The proportionally low level of participation of the members of the community in higher/professional education limits their competency, and this aspect affects their empowerment. The system tending to reinforce social inequality and class-based privileges is an obstacle to societal progress and community empowerment. It is obvious that leaving education service delivery largely to private sector is unlikely to reduce disparities in education attainment of the privileged elite groups and the disadvantaged sections.

The inability of an overwhelming majority of Muslim individuals to access equal opportunity in education and employment is a key factor responsible for their continued backwardness, powerlessness, helplessness and human development problems, and failure to take their place within mainstream society. Because of shortage of creative skills for their self-sufficiency and self-reliance, the graduates in the community gaining self-worth and capacity to change their social constructions and to handle life's problems on their own to achieve empowerment is limited. Education service in the privatisation context has not substantially helped the young to overcome this deficiency.

Very few students from backward segments in the Muslim community pursue higher education under private self-financing educational institutions by availing loans from banks. For the poor among the Muslim community dependence on bank loan for educational purposes is risky because of the uncertainty regarding employment prospects after completion of education. Those who make use of loan facilities for education are caught in indebtedness– a disempowerment phenomenon.

Public-private partnership in education supported by bank loans to finance students' education will result only unfair and inequitable distribution of education leading to exclusion of the poor backward sections from employment, participation in economic activities and social security schemes, the outcome being loss of dignity, loss of self-confidence and self-esteem.

The growth of the youth with the potential capabilities is not addressed by private education providers. It is evident from the large numbers of educationally qualified individuals living in frustration and difficulties because they are devoid of necessary, effective and creative skills to find employment to take control of their life. Except a few members of urban-based upper middle class sections, very few among the educated Muslims are employed in high income, high dignity and privileged positions in high profile public or corporate sector. In the matter of educated minority community members improving their economic status by gaining entry into coveted regular jobs or improving productivity and incomes in self-employment, there is no significant breakthrough. The ubiquitous new generation private self-financing professional colleges do seldom assure the graduates a sustainable and stable career with dignity, self-respect and decent salaries

Conditions of private sector do have only fringe elements to make an empowering experience for most poor, backward, powerless, marginalised minority Muslim students in Kerala. The system fails to stimulate creativity and broader perspective among its products and is hardly inclusive. In fact, privatisation of education hinders inclusive education and hence, community empowerment. Advantaged groups are reinforced in their pursuit of narrow self-interest, with little empathy with the poor. The culture of the lifestyle they develop different from that of the laymen in the civil society is not an enabling element to contribute towards community empowerment as it impinges on cooperation, individual and collective obligation towards common good and social cohesion which is essential for the empowerment of the poor backward sections.

The Muslim community as such has yet to develop creative skills for their self-sufficiency and self-reliance, attain the necessary wherewithal to gain control over its forward and upward mobility in the socio-economic and political sphere. It still lacks self-confidence and resilience but has to depend on government agencies and others for solution to problems. It is found mired in a state of powerlessness. The community displaying political ability to influence the authority is due to its political organisational power. The education the privileged sections gain and the intellect and skills they develop are not substantially used to address the numerous problems the community faces. It is not used to significantly transform individual empowerment to community empowerment. Community empowerment is hardly an agenda of the private sector. In fact, private provision of education is devoid of any community development/ empowerment orientation.

To sum up, it is obvious that a great extent of problems faced by Muslim households and community with regard to their empowerment cannot be solved and the goal of empowerment of the community is unachievable through the policy of privatisation of education alone.

Findings

In Kerala's plural society where social development is unequal and distribution of resources inequitable, each community has varying educational needs and desires. To provide proper and purposeful education to the backward Muslim minority community for its empowerment is a major challenge.

Opportunity to access education under private sector is not equally open to all. Opportunities available are not equally accessible to all. For the poor it is too hard to take advantage or overcome socio-economic hurdles. In the context of the entrenched socio-economic inequalities and elite class domination, private sector delivering education on market principles has the outcome of the privileged sections cornering disproportionate benefits. Competition and choice (associated with private sector), although free from student's competence and academic score, but attached to his purse, serves to advance narrow sectarian interests of the privileged classes and further aggravates inequalities in educational opportunities. This system results in hierarchically divisive education system that keeps the less privileged outliers disquiet. The system of education engendered by privatisation (hierarchical) entails inequality in education attainment and employment opportunities of people with different economic status. This system may further lead to the emergence of new social hierarchies of dominant classes and accelerate divisive social cleavages. Although the less privileged sections reap absolute benefits, it is less likely to reduce inequality in the community and society. This tends to vitiate the goal of community empowerment. Obviously privatisation of education thwarts the value system that public education entertains – equitable distribution of educational opportunities that opens the door to social and economic opportunities – which the students loses.

- Empirical data indicate that education is not always and definitely an empowering experience for most poor students, particularly of the backward minority Muslim community and hence the poor has less incentive for pursuit of higher education. Other factors are also involved. Despite the very significant change that has occurred in higher education sector in the State, the system has many areas of concerns like financing, management, access, equity, reorientation toward socio-economic progress, empowerment, justice etc.
- Since private and self-financing agencies operate educational institutions with profit-motive, the people of low earnings are not able to secure education to satisfy their needs and aspirations because common/public education is constrained in providing education of equitable quality. Under the system of private provision of education, the objective of delivering education services to members of previously powerless communities and develop their capacities remain crippled.
- Education under private sector, linked to economic privileges, puts a premium on the education and empowerment of the less privileged who, despite having high academic score, have to abandon their ambition for higher education. They encounter a situation in which affluent children, though are dumb and of poor academic

score, pursue education in good, well-resourced schools/colleges and manage to secure higher degrees.

- Privatisation/marketisation of education is touted to bring the benediction of private capital/finance investment to all, but in reality it rambles up on the poor, undermines their right to education and entitlements. There is significant shift in privileges away from the resourceless to the economically privileged/resourceful who acquire capacities because they can pay for private provision of education service. And privatisation promotes hegemony of those privileged classes. This is worrying and embarrassing and not helpful to community empowerment.
- Private provision of education in Kerala being elitist/privileged class-friendly barely helps socio-economic mobility of the poor within the Muslim community. Only a minority of professionally qualified Muslim individuals could achieve upward mobility to reach the level of advanced members of forward communities – an essential requirement towards empowerment. This situation keeps the community remain only on the rim of empowerment.
- Earning degrees after paying high fees will create inequality in society. Products of private sector education/training who parted with hefty amount for their education/training, and committed to recover the same barely contribute to the welfare of the community, and their public engagement hardly achieves community empowerment. Pursuit of professional education aimed at generating employment and more money and acquiring status is unlikely to contribute to empower the community.
- Higher fee paid graduates churned out by the different types of institutions would have little motivation to do good to others. An education service for which students have to bear the burden of cost is unlikely to inculcate ideal social relations to construct shared values that enrich and transform communities. The products of that service are less likely to act righteously in their social behaviour to develop cooperation and develop individual, collective and mutually complementary obligations that benefit the community in which they are members. Nonetheless, they

are likely to develop mutually hostile mindsets and identities which impede community empowerment.

– Contrary to the presumption by some theorists that the interest of the higher strata and middle-class is in congruent with the common interest of the society/ community, majority of respondents (68 per cent) insisted that there is no synergy between them (interest of higher strata and middle class with common interest). Enhancement of the quality of life of a privileged section of the community will not necessarily and will not always lead to the development of the community as such. The new generation of educated Muslim individuals do not succeed in contributing to collective social and community actions to facilitate community empowerment. Self-efficacy and individual ability attained does not largely transform into collective efficacy/community potential. Individual development also does not largely result in sustainable and stable community development. On the other hand, advantaged groups are reinforced in their pursuit of narrow self-interest, with little empathy with the poor.

– The present education system does not help all students to attain the potential to overcome alienation, marginalisation, helplessness and powerlessness and worthlessness and self-determine their life and become self-reliant. In this situation, the bane of powerlessness/ helplessness and low self-confidence under which the Muslim community used to reel are less likely to be removed through the education of the privileged sections by the self-financing private sector.

– The goal of making equal education facilities to all and making education inclusive face challenges as the policy of letting managements charge education is a threat to the provision of free and compulsory education, the most fundamental elements of the right to education, to all children.

– Under such conditions the problem of equity in society has been aggravating and the empowerment of the backward minority communities is unlikely to be strengthened.

The policy of privatisation of education surrenders to the logic of economics and banks on the advantages offered by the big corporate business groups, and in that process vitiates social justice, equality of opportunities and self-confidence among individual, and in fact, renders education subordinate to commercial values. This market-oriented education system that creates inequalities and fosters injustice is counter to the stated objectives of NEP.

The private professional institutions are hardly looked upon as centres of excellence/knowledge acquisition but of preparing and enabling centres for acquiring employment. The students of these institutions hardly ever develop intellect and build their identity.

Even while admitting many of the stark features of private sector, people, including poor and backward, largely show preference for education under private sector institutions. This is because public education failed to enlist public confidence.

Suggestions

- Minority communities need be empowered as self-sufficient members of the society and be mainstreamed by providing them with tools and opportunities to improve their quality of life. Free, accessible, inclusive and universal quality education that strives for excellence, innovation, creativity and knowledge and skills, the power of which affects life chances, is key to this and to prevent their perpetual powerlessness.
- Development of the Muslim community members with knowledge and skills that facilitate leadership and decision-making in order to enable them to advance careers in administration, judiciary, defence, police forces, science and technology, law etc. is central in their empowerment. Therefore, a new sort of Muslim leadership, in lieu of the present statusquoist and elitist one motivated by self-interest and venality, that would address the community's economic and educational marginalisation and help galvanise people's interest in educating their children, be promoted. This leadership having attained ability and resources will act on their own

purposes, values, feelings and meanings rather than on those they uncritically assimilate from others. This will help them to gain greater control over all aspects of their lives as socially responsible clear thinking decision makers–a key factor that helps in their empowerment.

- In the context of large inequity in terms of socio-economic inequalities and uneven privileges experienced by some segments affirmative action for ensuring inclusive educational development of the backward communities cannot be neglected. The situation of parents' wealth and education status (cultural capital) determining education attainment of children must be eliminated.
- Equal opportunities in all spheres of education and regular employment must be ensured to encourage, motivate and attract the students of Muslim community into the folds of formal education. The employment lag faced by the community could be mitigated to some extent with public investment in human capital. Education service providers should be encouraged to render services on philanthropic principles, and not for profit. Unaffordable fees and other direct costs imposed are disincentive in the pursuit of education and a deterrent factor that affects education and empowerment of the backward sections. An appropriate strategy to overcome economic barriers in accessing education must also be implemented.

Private provision of education to turn beneficial to the disadvantaged sections must be effectively overseen, monitored, supervised and its performance audited. Government-private cooperation and obligations as well as provision for stakeholders' participation in education programmes in the increasingly privatised ambience will yield positive outcomes in education service delivery to the poor. Since private provision of education is a reality, a new education policy setting forth a right combination of roles by public and private sectors for education with the goal of ensuring education as right rather than a privilege must be formulated and implemented. A new public-private relationship defined by cooperation and complementarities must be developed with a view to address the issues of responsiveness, equity as well as quality improvement in education.

- Government should continue to discharge its responsibility to the delivery of social goods – education, healthcare, housing etc. that will stimulate economic activity and job creation which is correlated to empowerment of the poor. Although, in the neo-liberal dispensation, when the State changes its role from one of being the principal vehicle for socio-economic development to one of guiding and facilitating that development, the State cannot absolve its responsibility towards provision of quality education to the poor, and hence there is need to increase allocation for education as a political priority. Enhancing a public-funded common school system, the government need to promote a rational system of public education free from market regulation to benefit all sections of society with equity, fairness and social justice, and ensure equitable educational and learning opportunities for all children. Since public education provides space for socialisation of varied sections the same is more suitable for community-building and therefore must be universalised. Public education to which the entire society has a stake need be made purposeful, inclusive and of good quality to facilitate empowerment. Public-funding through a system of predictable long-term financing for education is indispensable to promote the goal of equitable education, narrowing the gaps in educational endowments between different communities/classes of people, a core element to promote empowerment of the backward.
- Further the gap between government run and affluent private schools in the matter of infrastructure needs be bridged.

At a time when the processes of globalization and government policy make new demands on Muslim students, it is important to develop an education programme that researches community issues and train community members with contemporary knowledge of the world that brings the skills of higher education to them.

The education system must focus on inculcating values, fostering of mutual understanding, mutual respect, attitude of tolerance, stable and sustained intercommunity relations/ connections and harmonious and peaceful living – elements of empowerment of the minorities.

Educational institutions must be obligated to building and nurturing resilient, enduring and supportive community relations within communities against the contractual, hierarchical and impersonal relations that is now being engendered.

- Innovative programmes to enable the community to achieve social and economic mobility and progress and empowerment in life must be designed and implemented. The issue of socio-economic backwardness and inequality needs to be addressed with top priority if Muslim community as such is to progress educationally and to empower. In this respect, community-based targeting, instead of income-based targeting, alone will yield results by reducing its disadvantages which have historical and social reasons.
- Education for minorities must be sought within the agenda of equality in the State's economic, social and political spheres.
- Edúcated must develop a culture of common cause with fellow community members and work to bring about social change to facilitate community empowerment.
- Muslim students should have the feeling that they are equal participants and that they are not being discriminated against and are free from any feeling of prejudices in any institution. This is necessary to mitigate the problem of communalism, fascist behaviour, superior-inferior mindset, socio-economic inequalities and exclusion – all important towards empowerment.
- In the context of Muslim reassertion of its identity and culture, it is advisable that Muslim academic institutions are controlled and managed by the community as such rather than individuals, to focus on community culture and interest.
- Ways to reverse the trend of privatisation generating inequality in education attainment with all its dangerous social, economic and political consequences must be strengthened. The issue of socio-economic inequality and

inter community power imbalances needs to be addressed with top priority if Muslim community as such is to attain educational progress and empowerment. A fair basis for managing the inequalities requires promotion of equality of opportunities and strengthening the minimum requirements to which the minorities are entitled.

- A rational programme for deconcentration of educational facilities from urban centres to rural areas must be implemented to benefit rural poor.
- Enforcement of the RTE Act would act as a corrective to the free market-based privatisation and help in educational advancement of weaker sections.

Notes and References

1. See John Hurst (1997), "On Popular Education", National Lewis University, http://www.nl.edu/academics
2. Muslim population in Kerala constitute 24.2 per cent of the population of Kerala.
3. Amartya Sen, 1970, The Crisis in Indian Education, Lal Bahadur Sastri Memorial Lecture, March 10-11, 1970, quoted in S.C. Malik, Management and Organization of Indian Cities, Indian Institute of Advanced Study, Shimla, p. 259.
4. See also Krishna Kumar (2010), *op cit.*

Index